本书由大连外国语大学2015年学科
建设专项经费资助出版

百人学术文库

英语名词短语前置修饰语语序的认知研究

A Cognitive Study on the Order of Prenominal Modifiers Within English Noun Phrases

林　璐 / 著

新　华　出　版　社

图书在版编目（CIP）数据

英语名词短语前置修饰语语序的认知研究 / 林璐著．
北京：新华出版社，2018.4

ISBN 978-7-5166-4029-6

Ⅰ.①英… Ⅱ.①林… Ⅲ.①英语—名词—短语—修饰语—研究 Ⅳ.①H314.3

中国版本图书馆 CIP 数据核字（2018）第 077418 号

英语名词短语前置修饰语语序的认知研究

作　　者：林　璐

责任编辑：张　谦　　**封面设计：**中联华文

出版发行：新华出版社

地　　址：北京石景山区京原路 8 号　　**邮　　编：**100040

网　　址：http：//www.xinhuapub.com

经　　销：新华书店

购书热线：010-63077122　　**中国新闻书店购书热线：**010-63072012

照　　排：中联学林

印　　刷：三河市华东印刷有限公司

成品尺寸：170mm×240mm

印　　张：13　　**字　　数：**240 千字

版　　次：2018 年 5 月第一版　　**印　　次：**2018 年 5 月第一次印刷

书　　号：ISBN 978-7-5166-4029-6

定　　价：45.00 元

图书如有印装问题，请与印刷厂联系调换：010-89587322

Abstract

This study attempts to explore the ordering operations within noun phrases, with special reference to the orders of coordinate idioms and prenominal modifiers, in terms of iconicity principles. The fact that the orderings of coordinate idioms and prenominal modifiers are relatively rigid renders people to wonder: what is the main motivating factor behind such linguistic phenomena? Former scholars attempted to formulate rules by looking into the phonological and semantic aspects of coordinate idioms and prenominal modifiers. Though their findings successfully provided a proper description of the word order phenomena, they failed to support a plausible explanation for why the ordering is arranged in this way. Consequently, the present study attempts to dig out a valid and persuasive motivation for the order of all the premodifiers within an English noun phrase.

It is further believed that the ordering study of coordinate idioms and prenominal modifiers can be attributed to a cognitive approach because a cognition-based analysis stresses that human cognitive abilities are devoted to the structures of language. As a representative of cognitive linguistics, iconicity posits that there exists a natural relation between language and human experience, and that linguistic structure to certain degree mirrors human conceptual structure.

It is based on this view that the present study intends to analyze the order arrangement of modifying elements from an iconic perspective. As far as coordinate idioms are concerned, their fixed orders are arranged predictably. Based on the temporal and spatial order found via substantial English data, a proper conclusion is drawn that English coordinate idioms are to a considerable extent, iconic of the occurrence sequence of the events such as the order of natural phenomena, human experiential activities, and the egocentric, vertical and horizontal orders in space. It further verifies that those fixed expressions following the unmarked-marked or positive-negative orders are also oriented towards human conceptual structure. This is compatible with the sequential order principle: the linear sequence of linguistic structures iconically corresponds to the conceptual order it represents.

As far as the order of prenominal modifiers is concerned, English prenominal modifiers can be explained in terms of the distance principle on the condition that the proper motivating factors governing prenominal modifiers can be found. This study finds that semantic constraint and syntactic factor are two major determinants to explain the different distances of prenominal modifiers to their head noun. Based on Quirk et al's (1972) semantic features of adjectives, it is found that when a noun or a gerund premodifies its head, it will exhibit more noun-like semantic properties than other prenominal modifiers do, while a further analysis of (past and present) participles reveals that participles are syntactically more distant from the head noun than nouns, gerunds and adjectives because they retain more or less the semantic properties of their original verbs. In this sense, the linguistic distances of prenominal modifiers from the head noun reflect their conceptual distances to the head noun. These findings can be summarized into what is called "The Principle of Nouniness":

a. The more nominal properties a prenominal modifier has, the closer to the head noun.

b. The more adjective properties a prenominal modifier has, the less close to the head noun.

c. The more verbal properties a prenominal modifier has, the least close to the head noun.

In terms of this principle, the general order of prenominal modifiers are established as follows:

(Past and Present) Participles > *Adjectives* > *Denominal Adjectives* > *Nouns* > *Gerunds* > *HEAD NOUN*

Adjectives are the component members of premodifiers. However, a single polarity of being gradable/ungradable is not sufficient enough to order all types of adjectives. This study carefully selects six calibrations to carry out the gradability degree of adjectives. The intention is to gain a clearer comprehension of the distinction between adjectives by means of quantitative study of various adjective features. Judged from the six calibrations on the gardability level, the ordering tendency goes like the following:

a. the lower a prenominal adjective is in the gradability degrees, the closer to the head noun

b. the higher a prenominal adjective is in the gradability degrees, the more distant to the head noun.

The findings in this study have added solid evidence to Haiman's iconicity principles. This verifies that iconicity is plausible in explaining some word order issues at the phrasal level. It is also hoped that more discoveries of linguistic phenomena will be obtained under the iconic framework.

Keywords: premodifiers; iconicity; markedness; arbitrariness; motivation

Acknowledgments

First and foremost, I would like to express my deepest thanks to Professor Doo-Shick Kim, for his endless encouragement, patient attention, and generous help throughout the doctoral course study. In particular, the time of finishing the research, I cannot avoid the feeling of privilege to have had such a great supervisor. He has led and fostered my interests of iconicity in the field of linguistics. In the process of my research, he has given me many helpful and insightful suggestions for the problems I encountered. Needless to say, many enlightening ideas in the process of book-writing have been inspired from frequent contacts with him. His critical attitudes towards academic thinking have shown me the true meaning of a learned and experienced researcher by example. Without his support and guidance through the past these years, I could not have finished my research.

My thanks also extend to the other professors Byeong-Tae Moon, Se-Eun Jhang, Kwangho Lee and Sei-Rang Oh for their reading this book page through page and for their precise and useful comments. Professor Moon and Professor Lee encouraged me to consider the word order phenomena from a creative point of view. Without their inspiration, I might have missed the most essential value in my research. The suggestions from Professor Oh were the most instructive for the organization of the book and for filing up some logical gaps. Professor Jhang's correct comments fired me to narrow the topic of the writing to the word order within English noun phrases and he also patiently showed me how to revise the references.

My thanks also go to professor Byeong-kil Ahn for offering me chances to share my knowledge with the other scholars in Korea. I am thankful for his constant advice throughout the writing of this book.

Finally, I wish to express my sincere thanks to my parents for their endless love and speechless care for everything when I was absent in China. I am also greatly indebted to my husband. I thank for his financial support during the whole period of this work. He has been the best listener to my complaints. I appreciate his considerable understanding and encouragement whenever I am in difficulty.

List of Abbreviations

AFP	the Animated First Principle
FSP	Functional Sentence Perspective
MOD	Modifier
NTH	Natural Topic Hierarchy
NP	Noun phrase
Obj	Object
Past	past tense
Prep	Preposition
Subj	Subject
SOV	Subject/object/verb
SVO	Subject/verb/object
UG	Universal Grammar
TFP	the Theme First Principle
VOB	Verb-object Bonding
VP	Verb phrase

目 录
CONTENTS

CHAPTER ONE INTRODUCTION ······ 1

1.1. Motivations and scope of this research ······ 8

1.2. Research methodology and data collection ······ 10

1.3. Feasibility of iconicity in word order ······ 15

1.4. A brief sketch of the chapters ······ 19

CHAPTER TWO LITERATURE REVIEW ······ 20

2.1. Studies on word order at large ······ 22

2.2. Previous studies on the order of coordinate idioms ······ 30

2.3. Previous studies on the order of prenominal modifiers within a noun phrase ······ 36

2.4. Discussion and summary ······ 46

CHAPTER THREE THEORETICAL FRAMEWORK: ICONICITY AND ICONICITY PRINCIPLES ······ 49

3.1. Arbitrariness versus Iconicity ······ 50

3.2. Three principles of Iconicity ······ 59

3. 3. Summary ······ 69

CHAPTER FOUR AN ICONIC ANALYSIS OF WORD ORDER WITHIN COORDINATE IDIOMS ······ 71

4. 1. Definition and general properties ······ 72

4. 2. The analysis of coordinate idioms from Temporal Order Principle ······ 75

4. 3. The analysis of coordinate idioms from Spatial Order ······ 83

4. 4. An analysis of coordinate idioms from Markedness Order ······ 90

4. 5. Discussion and summary ······ 103

CHAPTER FIVE AN ICONIC ANALYSIS OF WORD ORDER WITHIN PRENOMINAL MODIFIERS ······ 106

5. 1. Definitions of modifiers within an English noun phrase ······ 107

5. 2. Classifications of modifiers ······ 109

5. 3. Linear order of determiners ······ 113

5. 4. Linear order of adjectivals as prenominal modifiers ······ 125

5. 5. Gradability degree of prenominal adjectives ······ 142

5. 6. Discussion and summary ······ 163

CHAPTER SIX CONCLUSION ······ 167

6. 1. Findings ······ 167

6. 2. Limitations and further work ······ 172

References ······ 174

CHAPTER ONE INTRODUCTION

The present study aims to investigate the word order[①] phenomena within English noun phrases. The key focus will be laid on the word orders within English coordinate idioms and the ordering of prenominal modifiers within an English noun phrase. In characterizing the observed order, however, linguists mostly appeal to the traditional distinction between free word order languages and fixed word order languages. As pointed out by Stucky (1981), English, notable for its explicit inflectional variations, is often cited as a prototypical example of fixed word order languages because superficially seen, word order in English is syntactically determined. Thus the fact that the orderings of all modifiers are relatively rigid inevitably renders people to wonder: what is the motivating factor behind such linguistic phenomena?

Earlier efforts into English word order issue from Maslkiel (1959), Cooper and Ross (1975) and Allan (1987) are mainly devoted to the formulation of rules by looking into the phonological and semantic aspects of coordinate idioms. However, people fail to rely on any explanation available from their accounts to recognize why coordinate idioms are ordered this way because their findings are only a descriptive demonstration of these linguistic phenomena. It is believed in the present study that the research into the coordinate idioms can be related or extend to a cognitive approach. That is, the or-

---

① Throughout the book, the expression *word order* is used as a cover term for both word order and constituent order. The distinction between the two terms will be discussed below in Chapter Two.

derings in some coordinate idioms are constrained rigidly because the organizations of some coordinate idioms can mirror the conceptual structures① that human beings gain from the experiential world, as is shown in the following example.

(1) a. (to put on) socks and shoes/ scissors and paste

b. here and there/ front and back

Former researchers tend to classify the types of coordinate idioms displayed in the example (1b) into the so-called "*here and front*" semantic domains (Cooper and Ross, 1975), but present no account for the type of coordinate idioms given in example (1a). It is interpreted in this study instead that the sequence of all the constituents in example (1a) is iconically arranged in the sense that the syntactic order corresponds to human experiential activities in real life (i. e. *putting on socks before shoes* and *using scissors to cut before pasting*), while that of the coordinate idioms shown in example (1b) are iconic in that they conform to spatial sequences which human beings perceive in the world: people conceive themselves the vantage point of the canonical situation of utterance, so the sequence "*here and there*" exists in language; people have their principal organs of perception directed towards the region in front of them, thus the more salient "*front*" direction precedes the less salient one denoted by the lexical form "*back*" (Lyons, 1979: 691). Seen in this principle, it is workable to explain that various aspects of linguistic structures within coordinate idioms are subject to the construal from human experiences and concepts in the world.

As far as prenominal modifiers are concerned, semantic classifications from both

---

① According to Croft and Cruse (2004:3), "conceptual structure cannot be reduced to a simple truth-conditional correspondence with the world. A major aspect of human cognitive ability is the conceptualization of the experience to be communicated (and also the conceptualization of the linguistic knowledge we possess) [⋯] In particular [⋯] grammatical constrictions play a major role in construing the experience to be communicated in specific ways."

English and Chinese scholars (Goyvaerts 1968, Hetzron 1978, Quirk et al 1985, Bache 1978, Dixon 1982, Gu 1986, Zhang 1998, among others) provide an appropriate description of the preferred ordering occurrence based on their semantic features. However, it is deficient in explaining the motivation causing the sequence. Their approaches assume that the ordering of prenominal modifiers has nothing to do with the head noun which is seen as the center of the noun phrase, though they admit that modifiers are only the constituents dependent on the head. However, the present study proposes that the ordering of prenominal modifiers cannot be explained without an investigation into the semantic properties of the head noun. Based on Haiman's conceptual closeness, it is observed that prenominal modifiers will be conceptually and linguistically closer to the head if they have more similar semantic properties to share with head noun. To put it another way, the linguistic distance between the center of a noun phrase and its modifiers reflects their semantic distance which is sequentially reflected by the conceptual distance. This study will introduce a cognition-based semantic analysis method to explain the problems at issue. In effect, a wide range of syntactic or semantic phenomena is able to be explored in the field of human cognitive concepts. This idea can be exemplified as follows:

(2) a. a *heated indoor swimming* pool

b. Washington's *oldest Italian grocery* store

In example (2), the head of the noun phrase "*pool*" semantically possess more nominal properties, thus it is syntactically classified in the domain of nouns. Given that our observation is true, modifiers that have more nominal semantic properties will syntactically stay closer to the head. Compared with the modifiers "*indoor*" and "*heated*", the nominalized word "*swimming*" has the maximal nominal properties, denoting it can be conceptualized that the pool serves the function of "swimming". Compared to the word "swimming", the modifiers "*indoor*", meaning that the pool is "inside of the house", indicates the location of the pool, containing also the semantic properties of prepositions. Similarly, the modifier "*heated*", meaning that the pool is "heated to become hot or warm", carries to certain degree, the verbal semantic properties, going distant to the head noun. Therefore, the modifier "swimming" takes the position the closest to the center noun; the word "indoor", more distant; but the adjective "heated", which is the modifier having the least nominal properties, takes the position the most distant from the head. In the same way, the order of the premodifiers illustrated in example (2b) can be well explained. It is this kind of conceptual identification that has greatly influenced the grammatical and semantic analysis of some word order phenomena. All these have clearly shown that word order is not arranged arbitrarily in that languages are characteristic of a syntagmatic organization of linguistic elements.

The present argument upon word order within English noun phrases accepts the notion that human conceptual mechanism can be dedicated to the form and meaning of language, as Langacker agreeably holds that language draws on more general cognitive systems and mental capacities from which it cannot be neatly separated (Langacker 2004). Implicit in this view is the assumption that linguistic structure reflects conceptual structure, which is represented by iconicity in language (Peirce 1940; Haiman 1985a, 1985b; Givón 1990, 1995). Along with the explanation of these linguistic phenomena, this study satisfies another purpose. The iconicity hypothesis, as a cognition-based analytical approach, is qualified as a basic and underlying theoretical framework that has an explanatory role in phrase-based word order facts.

Iconicity is defined as a natural linking between language phenomenon and human conceptualizations which are based on human cognitive experiences on the entities in the physical world. It insists that there exist a natural relationship between the form of the language and the meaning that the form denotes. The intuition behind iconicity is simple: the structure of language reflects in some degree the structure of human experience, that is to say, the structure of the world, including the perspective imposed on the world by the speaker (Croft 2000: 164).

The iconicity hypothesis rejects either the idea of merely stressing the formal relationship among grammatical elements independent of discoursal context, or the practice of heavily characterizing the extra-grammatically pragmatic properties of those elements independent of speaker's inner construal of situations. Since a property of language is characterized as iconic, the physical or diagrammatic form of language resembles its conceptual or discourse referents. Under the iconic framework, grammatical structures have to iconically reflect human conceptual structures. Therefore, speakers' mental options are associated with their grammatical choices structurally available in discourse. That is to say, iconicity principles govern speaker's choices of structurally available options in discourse. It can account for stable as well as dynamic characteristics of grammatical elements. A correlation of the rigid use of form and natural motivation of meaning in iconicity principles seems to have the greatest significance in the research concerning grammar. It can thus be claimed that iconicity principles take the lead in attempting to explain the distribution of typological features of the world's languages.

The discussion of the linguistic structure's correspondence to the conceptual structure mainly focuses on three aspects, which are entitled "three principles of iconicity" here. The first aspect is concerned with the linear order of linguistic elements, which is the so-called "Sequential Order Principle". It announces that the sequence of linguistic elements or structures can iconically conform to the order of the occurrence of the depicted events. This feature is obviously present in Caesar's famous Latin phrase: "Vēnī, vīdī, vīcī." meaning "I came, I saw, I conquered." The three clauses can never be distorted because they are viewed as iconic of the scenes of our experience in which the events occurred in a temporal order.

In addition, linguistic structures can reflect conceptual structures in the sense that the complex concept needs a complex linguistic expression, which is entitled as Quantity Principle by Givón(1989). This principle can be illustrated as below.

(3) a. *He ran.*

b. *He ran, ran, ran and ran.* (Kim 2004: 11)

What sentence (3a) implies is merely an action of the subject "*he*". However, the linguistic form becomes complex as shown in the second sentence in which the verb "*ran*" is repeated as many as four times. The repetition of the verb form within the sentence (3b) implies that additional meaning is supplied here. It is all agreed that the meaning of sentence (3b) parallels to that of the sentence: *He ran continually.*

The last aspect of iconicity helps to account for the fact that things which belong to a single category conceptually tend to be put together linguistically, which is called Distance/Proximity Principle (Haiman 1985). Coordination facts can show that this idea is at work. Consider:

(4) a. the ability to read and to write the letter

b. the ability to read and write the letter (Bolinger 1977: 7)

According to Bolinger (1977), the semantic relationship between the verbs "*read*" and "*write*" is closer in (4b) than that in (4a) in that they seem to share the same direct object "*letter*" in (4b), but it is not the case in (4a). The absence of preposition "*to*" after the coordinator "*and*" in (4b), iconically reflects the closeness in meaning between the two verbs "*read*" and "*write*".

The current study is grounded on viewing language forms from an iconic perspective. The position of the study is that linguistic structure mirrors human conceptual or experiential structure and that linguistic meaning is derivable to a considerable degree from linguistic form which is closely related to human conceptual structures. As far as word order phenomena are concerned, any word order variant can cause a subtle difference in meaning, which is supposed to be explained in terms of human cognitive experience in the real world.

The iconicity principles up to now have risen to treat a bulk of linguistic phenomena, ranging from phonological and lexical to sentential and discoursal levels. In retrospect, it is understandable because iconicity survives out of the struggle against arbitrariness. Saussure (1983) proposes his idea of arbitrariness and explains very clearly that the arbitrary nature in language is restricted to the lexical level. Naturally, the challenge from scholars has promptly rebuked this view by showing that language is actually motivated at the lexical level (Anttila and Embleton 1994; Sadowski 2001; Anderson 1998).

A deeper investigation into linguistic structures makes another assumption come to fruition. That is, language is greatly motivated at the syntactic level (Haiman 1983; Bybee 1985; Givón 1994; Fischer 1999). Nowadays an extensive body of researchers double their efforts in challenging "Saussure's arbitrariness" by showing how iconicity influences at the discoursal level (Enkvist 1981, 1989; Müller 1999; Tabakowska 1999; Wolf 2001). Examples can be easily found in dative movement, particle movement, subject-verb inversion, and so on. Unfortunately, few studies (Fischer 2001; Conradie 2001) can be referred to when the linguistic phenomena at the phrasal level are dealt with from an iconic perspective. Even fewer touch on the word order within noun phrases, such as coordinate idioms and prenominal modifiers. To my knowledge, only in the edited book *The Motivated Sign*, Fischer (2001) and Conradie (2001) have respectively studied the phrasal structures on the position of adjectives and S- and OF-genitives in English under the theoretical framework of iconicity.

Owing to the scarcity of research in iconicity on this respect, the present study confines the research scope to the word order phenomena within noun phrases with the intention of highlighting the explanatory role of iconicity at the phrasal level. In doing so, iconicity can further manifest its plausibility in wider linguistic scopes. The conclusion of this demonstration is that by means of a study of the word order within coordinate idioms and prenominal modifiers in English or Chinese, some iconicity principles can be implemented in the explanation of some word order phenomenon within noun phrases.

In the rest of this chapter, the motivations for and scope of the research, data collection and methodological issues will be mentioned first. After a brief description of the theoretical base for word order, a chapter outline is presented.

1.1. Motivations and scope of this research

There are two factors that motivate the present thesis. The first is to exhibit that what cannot be solved in the formalist approach① can find its answer in cognitive linguistics. The present approach can be viewed as a supplementary work to formalists including both Saussure and Chomsky traditions. Saussure maintains that grammar is an arbitrary and self-contained formal system of rules. Based on generative grammar②, Chomsky's view is that linguistic universals are manifestations of human's innate language-specific faculty, which is modularized and independent of other cognitive systems. This language-specific faculty is characterized by Chomsky in his Universal

① The formalist approach is one of the two orientations in modern linguistics: it focuses centrally on linguistic form. In the early 1960s, Chomsky and his associates started using the word "structuralist" to refer to those form-centered models that preceded generative grammar, in particular, to those in the American post-Bloomfield tradition. It seems that the term "structuralist" is a substitute for "formalist".

② Some linguists (Bates and MacWhinny 1989, Traugott 1985) express lucidly against generativists, because they believe that grammar is immune to external influence. However, Newmeyer (1998b:158 – 159) argues that most of them have misinterpreted Chomsky's views and insists that the module of Universal Grammar has a partly functional motivation and that Chimsky also involves "considerations of language use".

Grammar, which consists of inborn sets of principles and parameters.

It is of course reasonable to assume that there is a significant innate component and that some of the innate properties give rise to human language abilities. However, innateness of cognitive abilities has not been a chief concern of cognitive linguists, who are more concerned with demonstrating the role of general cognitive abilities in language. Much of their research has been devoted to elucidating conceptual structures as they are seen to apply to language. They insist that form should not be independent of its meaning, but mostly, if not entirely, derived from meaning. As Langacker (1993: 1) pinpoints that "language structure furnishes important clues concerning basic mental phenomena". Tai (1995: 2) agrees that "genuine explanations lie in both the structures of the real world, as conceptualized by the language user, and the linearity of human speech." In other words, linguistic explanations should be processed in terms of humans' perceptual and cognitive structures.

Although this motivation does serve as the main inspiration for this work, it should be clearly noted that the achievement of the challenge is far beyond the scope of a single thesis and continuously extensive work is needed before such an ambition is achieved. Instead, the aim of this study is to provide a baseline for the task which can serve as a common framework for future work in this field.

The second motivation is to provide the evidence that the application of Haiman's iconicity principles is plausible in word order issues at phrasal level. After the realization that a rigidly modularized description is unconvincing to account for certain linguistic phenomena, a scientific and natural-sounding extra-linguistic theory is called for to solve the problem. In recent years, researchers have witnessed the development of the iconic approach. In particular, the three principles of iconicity have enabled to explain and help better understand considerable syntactic structures. However, word order issues within noun phrases have been left a periphery of iconic theory. The goal of this study is to bring them to the attention of contemporary researchers.

This study is concerned with the question of what factors motivate word order within coordinate idioms and the prenominal modifier order within noun phrases. In particular, the explanation attempts to render the conclusion that human experiential activities, human perceptions of the nature and the world, as well as human cognitive propensity govern the human preference for the orderings of both coordinate idioms and prenominal modifiers.

For obvious reasons, not all the word order phenomena within noun phrases can be covered here. What this book will do is deliberately narrow the topic to two typical word order phenomena: the orderings of coordinate idioms and prenominal modifiers within noun phrases, which can exhibit interesting analytic problems and to infer from the current study how other word order phenomena are explained in terms of the iconicity principles. These two linguistic phenomena are so tricky that many grammarians are determined to ascribe them to the grammatical rules. This study instead, shows that the explanation of their motivation can be well achieved by exploring into human conceptual structures and cognitive mechanisms. In turn, the realization of the close correlation between language and human conceptualization in the real world can help people profoundly comprehend and acquire linguistic structures.

1.2. Research methodology and data collection

The data employed here are in a large part based on published written formal texts of naturally occurring tokens culled from a variety of authentic linguistic, literary, journalistic sources including two on-line publications: *Washington Post* and *Newsweek*.

Two crucial determinants affect the way of data collection. First, since iconicity explanation relies to a large degree on the natural, physical or experiential world, naturally-occurring expressions are more persuasive than those made-up sentences. Second, all the data are deliberately culled from written sources for the reason that the concern of this study is canonical word order phenomena which most probably occur in written standard materials. Those non-canonical word order variants, constantly occurring in spoken informal expressions for specific communicative purposes, are excluded from this study. The data sources are all authoritative enough to guarantee the occurrence of the canonical word order phenomena involved. Coordinate idioms are good cases in point. While the order of the two conjuncts in some coordinate idioms cannot be reversed in many instances, a number of other cases exist in which the order of the two conjuncts is not fixed when the elements occur in non-idiomatic constructions.

(5) (Fore and aft/ * Aft and fore), kids are playing.

(Kids are playing at the front and the stern of the boat.)

(6) a. Both (cat and mouse/ mouse and cat) were exhausted after the chase.

b. Tip never plays (cat and mouse/ * mouse and cat) with Teddy.

(Tip never treats Teddy sometimes cruelly, or at other time kindly.)

It is obvious that the order of the two conjuncts in example (5) is always fixed. If reversed, the sentence is ungrammatical. However, the elements "*cat*" and "*mouse*" in example (6a) can be reversed at random without changing the meaning of the sentence. We regard it as non-idiomatic construction. Contrary to the example (6a), the order of the two components in example (6b) is fixed and we cannot predict the meaning of the idiom from their individual elements (i. e. the meaning of the coordinate idiom in example (6a) is different from that shown in example (6b)).

Only when the order of the two conjuncts within a construction is fixed and cannot be reversed can the construction be considered as an idiom. Since the topic of this study is on the ordering of coordinate idioms, the non-idiomatic constructions with reversible orders like example (6a) will be excluded in the course of data collection.

Two methodological issues need to be paid heed to. First of all, it has been mentioned that research into word order has been cast to the periphery of generative grammarians (Kuh 1990). In retrospect, this state of affair is excusable in that English, notable for its rigid word order, has served as the main language of exemplification for theory construction in most current syntactic frameworks. It is by no means an easy job to discover a universal grammar to account for widespread features of languages. When the disadvantage is recognized, they broaden the data beyond English and several other Indo-European languages. However, as more languages are involved, it becomes evident that languages show considerable variations. The problems with this Anglocentric orientation in theorizing about syntax have become obvious: while English-based syntactic theories are able to account for many widespread syntactic features of languages (e. g. , unbounded dependencies of various sorts), they are poorly equipped to deal with other syntactic features that are equally widespread but not manifested in English. ①

For fear of the reoccurrence of the same embarrassment, this study employs a typologically grounded database showing various degrees of word order in two languages: English and Chinese. This is done because once the principles are proposed but do not apply to even the neighbouring language, they cannot be considered as linguistic universals. It is further argued that a cross-linguistic tendency for the data collection can help to provide accounts for world-wide syntactic features in languages. The benefit of the typological methodology is that it contributes to the theory of universal grammar in ways that single-language analysis cannot. The primary goal of typological study is to demonstrate how some sort of expressive functions in different languages are achieved through different ways in different forms. All languages are compared in the search for those that

① See Zwicky (1986) for a list of the syntactic phenomena well represented in English as well as those that are poorly represented.

are universal; meanwhile comparison can be conducted for the differences. ① While comparing languages to determine "universal laws", typological study is also concerned to learn "about the general characteristics of humanity" (Meillet 1970: 13).

Moreover, as far as language typology is concerned, word order is a significant mechanism for language analysis. For example, owing to the lack of inflectional variations, Chinese depends extensively on word order to deliver semantic meaning in a sentential format. Though English is remarkably characteristic of its fixed word order, the single fixed word order becomes insufficient to cover various semantic and pragmatic aspects in human communication. It follows that a variety of word order variants are developed to indicate the change in meaning. Therefore, different reasons generate the same phenomena of word order variations. However to what extent they can be explained typologically remains to be seen. Examples appear below:

(7) a. a newly-built house (English)

b. 一座新建的房子 (Chinese)

c. *ein* (a) *neu* (newly) *gebautes* (built) *Haus* (house) (German)

(8) a. here and there; past, present and future (English)

b. 这里 那里;过去 现在 将来(Chinese)

c. ikot jeokot (here and there), eoje oneul naeil (past, present and future) (Korean)

It is clearly seen that the orders of prenominal modifiers in (7) and the orders of coordinate idioms shown in (8) are not only consistent in English and Chinese, but also in other languages, like German and Korean. Discoveries from researchers have amounted to more devotion: without an extensive investigation of data elicited from natu-

① Very few linguists with typological interests are content to describe generalization governing the distribution of linguistic elements in the language of the world. They go beyond description and explain the frequency and distribution. Indeed, many consider the tasks of ascertaining and explaining typological variants as inseparable.

ral speech, it will be inappropriate to offer evaluating arguments in favor of iconicity. Therefore, not immersing themselves in the powerful intuition about iconic organization of linguistics, researchers should instead count on various kinds of cross-linguistic word order patterns to yield useful universal generalizations. The report from a study of both English and Chinese can help to pave the way to some useful generalizations in word order.

In the process of providing accounts for the existence of word order variations in the two languages, it is not satisfactorily done with the idea that conclusions drawn in this study are merely limited to both languages. It is expected that the findings will be useful to launch later explorations into other languages for pertinent language universals. It should be enumerated that typological methodology is the most important way in which our most general conclusions are anticipated.

Second, a fresh attitude should be developed towards word order issues. Word order cannot be uniformly squeezed into a single theory or one principle. It is assumed that while one principle is the primary motivation in the determination of word order, other factors are accessible to and competing against it. When one motivation has greater influence over another, the language exemplifies a linguistic variation. A good case in point comes from the order of the following coordinate idioms:

(9) a. to put on *socks and shoes*

b. to put on *shoes and stockings*

It is observed that the order of example (9a) is iconic of human experiential activities (i. e. *putting on the socks before the shoes*), while the example (9b) is not necessarily the case. In the latter one, the iconic order has lost its competition against the phonological preference for monosyllables over disyllables in English. This may also be a good explanation for the apparent arbitrariness which probably arises from the competition between two equally motivated principles.

1.3. Feasibility of iconicity in word order

Earlier attempts to study word order are mainly centered on communicative dynamism. As defined by Firbas (1964: 270), the communicative dynamism of a linguistic element is "the extent to which the sentence element contributes to the development of the communication, to which, as it were, it pushes the communication forward." Within this framework, it is claimed that it is not the grammatical roles of the sentence elements, but rather their degree of communicative dynamism, that serves as the fundamental word ordering principle within the sentence with a dominant pattern in which *themes* tend to appear earlier *rhemes* in the sentence. The principle predicts the choice between sentence pairs like those shown in the example (10).

(10) a. He walked across the room and *gave the package to Mary.*

b. He walked across the room and *gave Mary the package.*

(Downing and Noonan 1995: 13)

Cowan (1995: 29-50) explains that given a discourse containing information about the *package* (*i. e.* the theme), but not about *Mary*, reader tends to choose sentence (10a) as the preferred completion to the sample discourse.

However, since the 1970s some researchers (Creider 1977, Tomlin and Rhode 1979, Mithun 1995, Payne 1995) have explored a diversity of languages in which the opposite order of communicative pattern (i. e. "*rhemes before themes*" order) is used for the purpose of delivering information. How is it possible that two distinct or completely opposite patterns are motivated in language use? The question remains unanswered in this field.

Recently, cognitive linguists argue that if it is the case that our understanding of a text is dependent on the increasing elaboration of a cognitive representation of the information carried by the text, it makes sense that those different communicative patterns correlate with the propensities of the human cognitive apparatus, or as it is claimed that distinct patterns are cognitively motivated. Because cognitive linguistics sees language as embedded in the overall cognitive capacities of human beings, topics of special interest for cognitive linguistics are the structural characteristics of natural language categorization such as prototypicality, cognitive models, the conceptual principles of linguistic organization like iconicity, namely naturalness, the experiential background of language-in-use, and the relationship between language and thought, including questions about relativism and conceptual universals.

Thanks to this point of view, scholars have begun to apply the iconicity theory to word order investigations. Referring to Jellinek (1913 – 14), Firbas first recognizes the iconic relations between the order of the expression in language and the natural order of the phenomena in real life. Although he has not pointed it out so explicitly as Langacker (1987b) and Tai (1989), Firbas (1992) does bring forth an important view in dealing with word order phenomena in general:

> "[...] language does not invariably follow the orders of the extra-linguistic reality. It is not a slave to this reality. Owing to an interplay of means, controlled by the immediate communicative concern and purpose of the speaker, language is capable of approaching the extra-linguistic reality from different angles and viewing it in different perspectives (p. 139)."

His remarks have two major implications for word order research. On one hand, the pervasive patterns of word order demonstrated in expressions of linguistic structures show that grammar is to a great extent iconicity-motivated. That is, the orderings of language are the real-time perception and production of a temporal sequence of discrete, structured symbolic units. Word order, on the other hand, is also conceptual-based because cognitive processes govern language use, in particular, the construction and communication of meaning by language. That is to say, categories and structures in semantics, syntax, and even morphology and phonology are built up from our cognition of specific utterances on specific occasions of use. The general conceptual principles constitute important structural principles in language.

In his famous *Natural Syntax*, Haiman (1985a) investigates a considerable number of linguistic structures to provide support for his claim that differences in form must reflect differences in meaning. In other words, form is iconic of its meaning. Haiman's evidence for language iconicity involves such linguistic structures as conditionals, possessive relationships, and coordination structures as well.

What follows is the view held by Langacker (1991b), that is, language is a symbolization of the conventionalized conceptual world. Language is not a direct reflection of the real world, but corresponds at an abstract level to "the language user's experience of the extra-linguistic reality" (Firbas 1992: 139) and conditioned by the language user's communicative purpose. This viewpoint amounts to the contention that the structure of language iconically mirrors the structure of concept, rather than independent properties of the unconscious mind, namely, the textual structure of language reflects in some way the conceptual processing construction of human experience or the structure of the world, including the perspective imposed on the words by the speaker.

Although iconicity has been discussed from upon a great deal of linguistic phenomena, it does not seemingly illustrate word order issue. In effect, Haiman, more than one time in his book, mentions the correlation between iconicity and word order. Haiman (1985a: 49) believes that the coordinate clauses must observe "tense iconicity": the order of clauses must correspond to the order of events, then perhaps the same is true of the usual order of conditional clauses, in which the protasis precedes the apodosis. Haiman (1985a: 253) even predicts that "perturbations of word order, even in so-called "free word order languages" like Hungarian or Russian, signal differences in meaning". Tai (1985) has voiced that in Chinese, the temporal order of the constituents is often a grammaticalization of the temporal order of the notions that they encode.

There seems to be a tendency to label the functional motivation for word order as iconic. Indeed, many word order phenomena in language have qualified themselves as iconically motivated. Let us take as an exemplification of iconicity the fact that the orders of coordinate idioms correlate with the natural sequence or human perceptual sequences of the events, as shown in the following example.

(11) the President and the Dean

Jakobson (1971a: 350) explains that "the order of speech events tends to mirror the order of narrated events in time or in rank." Thus, the sequence of the two nominal phrases in the example (11) is more acceptable than the reversed order by both speaker and the listener in that the tendency of human conceptualization seems to be that the order of inter-linguistic expression reflects the extra-linguistic factor of the ranking of official status according to which the higher occupational position is usually mentioned before the lower one.

Language is not a group of words ordered at random, but rather a system of grammatical rules to express complex concepts. This system of grammatical rules is our concern in that it reflects the properties of the world or human perceptions of the world. When we talk about word order, we expect to find answers in agreement with our conceptual structure. Iconic theory is compatible with the cognitive conceptualization of reality. As Givón (1985: 189) notes that "all other things being equal, a coded experience is easier to store, retrieve, and communicate if the code is maximally isomorphic to the experience". The prediction in this thesis is whether within the grammar of a single language or cross-linguistically we can find analogous effects with semantic dependence and word ordering principles. If the prediction is a success, iconicity principles can be an important factor in giving rise to corresponding word order.

1. 4. A brief sketch of the chapters

The proceeding chapters attempt to explain the motivational mechanisms of the word order phenomenon implicitly reflected in coordinate idioms and prenominal modifiers within English noun phrases in terms of Iconicity Principles proposed by Haiman. Chapter Two critically discusses previous accounts of word order within coordinate idioms and prenominal modifiers in English noun phrases with special focus cast on the merits and demerits of previous theories applied in the two word order phenomena. Chapter Three offers an overview of iconicity literature. It explicates the explanatory power of the three iconicity principles that will be applied in the present study. Chapter Four supplies a detailed and explanatory analysis of word order motivations in English and some of Chinese coordinate idioms. Meanwhile, the interplays of the iconic motivation, conceptual mechanisms and conventional constraints in coordinate idioms are discussed. Chapter Five provides a close examination of the motivating factors underlying the sequence of English prenominal modifiers in noun phrases. Chapter Six presents a summary of the findings in the research. It also points out the limitations of the present study and suggests possible avenues for further work.

CHAPTER TWO LITERATURE REVIEW

Over the past decades or so, much work has been done in terms of the determinant factors or principles that will probably influence the word order of a phrase or the whole syntactic structures in a language. The primitive efforts have been put on the typological descriptions of the relative frequency or distribution of the three basic constituent orders in a transitive clause, such as SVO or SOV, from such scholars as Greenberg (1963), Hawkins (1983), Mallinson and Blake (1981), Dryer (1984), and among others. The one that cannot be neglected is Greenberg who published his book entitled *Universals of Language* in 1966, observing that the actually occurring word order variability across languages comprises the orderings of constituents. His implicational universals represent an initial explanation for the limitations of constituent ordering in a clause. The impact of the book is considerable to such an extent that word order universals have received attention in a variety of linguistic fields. Hawkins (1983) conducts the follow-up research by expanding Greenberg's database and making diachronic predictions of the implicational and distributional universals.

From the beginning of the 1980s, some linguists began to provide explanations about word order variations as the result of functional principles of linguistic organization. The functional perspective has been developed in those major works contributed by Chafe (1976), Givón (1979, 1985), Dik (1978), Foley and van Valin (1984), Halliday (1985), Tomlin (1986) and Nuyts and Schutter (1987). They devote themselves to the explanation of the relative frequency to be the result of the interaction of functional principles. Though they uncover much useful information that contributes to our understanding of the specific discourse-forming functions, their explanatory principles are confined to a communicative system regardless of the fact that speakers' grammatical choices also depend on their conceptual construals of situation. However, many functional researchers (Downing and Noonan 1995, Newmeyer 1998b) questioned their theoretical restrictions by stating that word order choices may be dictated by the need of the speaker or writer to communicate in a way which is optimally matched to human's cognitive capacities. And it is a credence currently adhered to by cognitive linguists that language form is based on human experience and their conceptual processing towards the entities in the physical world.

Following the insightful researches mentioned above, semantic researchers (Cooper and Ross 1975, Givón 1984, Li and Thompson 1975, Malkiel 1968, Ransom 1979, Siewierska 1988, Allan 1987) tend to blend semantic accounts into functional explanations. Unlike the former researchers who merely confine to the topic of the three basic constituent orders, they take into considerations a majority of specific linguistic constructions like noun phrases, dative movement and idiomatic phrases but unfortunately not from a cognitive perspective.

Their contributions inspire more linguists to investigate various word order variations in terms of functional and pragmatic positions. Such scholars include de Schutter (1987), Wakker (1987), Downing and Noonan (1995) and so forth. At that time, cognitive views only stayed in the shadow and received less attention due to the popularity of functional approach. Despite that, some endeavors have been bravely executed, though they are usually the target of criticism from functionalists. In his work of mental models, Johnson-Llaird (1983) provided a general cognitive framework for understanding language within psychology and linguistics. For others, Krupa (1982), Pullum (1977) and Diehl (1975) were inevitably referred to.

The intention of this chapter is to address the above-mentioned approaches and then present how the word order within coordinate idioms and prenominal modifiers in an English noun phrase have been studied in literature. It is necessarily the case that their possible limitations will be pointed out.

2. 1. Studies on word order at large

Broadly speaking, word order is "the arrangement of words in a sentence, clause, or phrase to convey meaning. Some languages have relatively free word order: meaning is not changed by a change in the position of a word unless an emphasis is considered. Other languages have relatively fixed word order: meaning is changed or is not conveyed when the position of a word is changed" (Crowell 1964: 423).

Before moving on, it is vital to distinguish the term *word order* from that of *constituent order*. Word order (Kuh 1990: 190) actually refers to the order among the words within phrasal constituents, while the constituent order is frequently defined as the order principles directing how the major sentential constituents within syntactic fields are arranged for. In the narrow sense, it can be generalized as the ordering of morphemes and words; in the broad sense, it includes the ordering of linguistic constituents at various levels. In this research, the terminology *constituent order* can be designated to cover the senses of both *word order* and *constituent order*.

Strictly speaking, word order is different from constituent order. However, there are also cases that word order and constituent order overlap. Provided that sentences are constructed by words strung together, it is possible to conceive of a language in which the movement of major sentential constituents can switch the positions of the words within them, and thus meaning change will be caused. The language bearing this type of element movement is labeled by linguists as fixed constituent or word order language. And some grammars can also be investigated from both perspectives of the word order and constituent order, like prenominal modifiers and post-nominal modifiers in English. It is due to this profound interaction between word order and constituent order that this thesis chooses to use word order as a cover term for both types of orders. The history of word order study is not a long one, but it does leave a mark on the grammatical theories.

2.1.1. Typological descriptions

In earlier studies of Generative Grammar, research into word order is scattered in the circle of linguistics because Chomsky dismisses the rules that account for word order as being "not so much rules of grammar as rules of performances" (Chomsky 1965: 127). This is excusable because English, as mentioned above, is the key language of exemplification for theory construction at that time. English-based syntactic theories are successful to account for some widespread word order phenomena of languages, but they are unable to deal with other intriguing phenomena that are equally widespread but not explicitly manifested in English.

A cross-linguistic tendency for the data collection enables to produce accounts for world-wide syntactic features in languages. Thus some typologists (Greenberg 1966, Hawkins 1983, Mallinson and Blake 1981, Dryer 1984, Hale 1981) employ a typologically-grounded database showing various degrees of word order variations in languages to dig out the syntactic attributes in languages. Thanks to those scholars (Hale 1981, Hawkins 1983) who have brought the description of relatively unknown but prototypical free word order languages to our attention, we have now a relatively large database of languages showing various degrees of word order variations, and some of these languages have been given analyses under a variety of theoretical frameworks. Nevertheless, the research in this field is at too early a stage to amount to the utmost rigors of language universals. Furthermore a moment's thought of these investigations can reveal their problems within this traditional background.

Four decades ago, when he first observed the six possible orderings of the three nuclear constituents in a transitive clause, Greenberg (1963) stated his word order universals using implicational statements, and these paved the way for the discovery of other implicational universals. However, he just provided typological summary of the relative frequencies or distributions of various basic constituent order types, as shown in (12):

(12) SOV = SVO > VSO > VOS = OVS > OSV

Though the implicational universals have kept being expanded and enriched by successive typological linguists (Hawkins 1983, Dryer 1984), neither the preliminary job nor the subsequent work has provided a satisfactory answer to the simple question: how are those frequencies or distribution explained? Mallinson and Blake (1981) try to assert that word order facts can be accounted for according to three general principles, which are given as follows:

(13) Mallinson and Blake's three principles:

(a) More topical material tends to come nearer to the beginning of the clause than non-topical material.

(b) Heavy material tends to come nearer to the end of the clause than light material…

(c) Constituents tend to assume a fixed position in the clause according to their grammatical status or semantic relation or category status. (p. 151)

Seen from the viewpoint of current researches, the three principles proposed by both Mallinson and Blake imply a functional explanation, though they do little to highlight it. For instance, the principle in (13a) mentions that "more topical material tends to come nearer to the beginning of the clause", which accidentally coincides with the topic-comment opinion① in functional linguistics. Furthermore, as the mainstream of study at that time is still the order of the three basic constituents, their discussion is left only partially specified. In other words, the second and the third principles can not only help explain the order of the three basic constituents within a clause, but also other kinds of order variations within a sentence. However, sufficient or explicit explorations on it are not received from then on.

2.1.2. (Typological-) Functional accounts

The first explanation to the topic of the word order is developed by functional linguists, which is grounded on typological-functional principles. The major works are contributed by Chafe (1970), Chafe and Nichols (1986), Givón (1979, 1985), Dijk (1978), Foley and van Valin (1984), Halliday (1985) and Tomlin (1986), and among others. Under the theoretical background of social function explanations they attribute the word order determinant to the interaction of functional principles: the Theme First Principle (TFP), Verb-object Bonding (VOB), Natural Topic Hierarchy (NTH) and the Animated First Principle (AFP) (Tomlin 1986).

A principle like TFP proposed by Dane (1974) is an attempt to make more precise and explicit the idea that "old" information precedes "new" information. Thematic information concerns the focus on the important or salient information, ultimately requiring considerations of its connection to attention (Tomlin 1985, 1986). The essential claim embodied by VOB is that the object of a transitive verb forms a more cohesive syntactic and semantic whole than a transitive verb and its subject do. The principle of

① According to Kim (1999:197), the history of topic-comment idea probably begins with a non-European analog of theme-rheme of Functional Sentence Perspective (FSP) theory in Prague school. Hockett (1958) makes a distinction between the topic and the comment in a sentence, in that "the speaker announces a topic and then says something about it …[In English and the familiar languages of Europe], topics are usually also subjects and comments are predicates. (1958:201)"

AFP can be found in the work of linguists like Hyman and Hawkinson (1975) while Natural Topic Hierarchy (NTH) involves aspects of both agency and animateness. In addition, it has been claimed by Givón (1979) that all languages found SOV parent stocks sufficiently far back in time. Givón's evidence comes from diachronic analysis of word order change in Bantu language, where he observes grammatical fossils of SOV type in language which are uniformly SVO (Tomlin 1986: 6).

Around the same time, other linguists (Li 1976, Li and Thompson 1976, Hopper and Thompson 1980, Tomlin 1986) have conducted a great many profound studies in specific languages. The collaborative efforts of Bates and MacWhinney (1978, 1981, 1982) and Kintsch and van Dijk (1978) elaborate the functional approach within psychology.

From the beginning of the 1980s, some linguists began to account for word order through functional grammar. Functional linguists like Mathesius (1942, 1975) and Firbas (1992) hold that word order is a system governed by the mutual relations of word order principles, including grammatical principles, functional sentence perspective principles, emphasis and sentence-rhythm principles. Accounts from Firbas (1992: 118) hold that grammatical principles include both the principle of grammatical function and the principle of coherence of members. The functional perspective arranges sentence elements in a Theme-Transition-Rheme sequence in terms of information flow. The principle of emphasis is a pragmatically-motivated principle from the producer's point of view through ordering the elements within a sentence in a way that strikes the recipients as more or less out of the ordinary. The principle of sentence rhythm determines the stress patterns in spoken language.

These linguists fully recognize the importance of the impact of the interplay on the determination of word order to fulfill specific communicative purposes. However, they view different linguistic levels (i. e. grammatical, functional and prosodic levels) as unrelated, self-contained, autonomous domains. This leads to the constraints on their further investigation. Moreover, their explanatory principles focus too much on the function of communicative purposes, independent of speaker's identification of his/her inner cognitive capacities. Nowadays many functional researchers (Downing and Noonan 1995; Newmeyer 1998a, 1998b) mention that word order choices may be dominated in a way that corresponds to the mental choices from human conceptual or experiential world, so to speak, language form is based on human experience to the physical world and the conceptualization towards it.

2.1.3. Semantic-functional accounts

Efforts from functional pioneers have been concentrated on the possible ordering of the three basic sentence constituents, other than those parts of speech that have other grammatical category status (noun, verb and prepositional phrases, etc). Creative investigations have also been opened with regard to semantics by some linguists (Cooper and Ross 1975, Givón 1984, Li and Thompson 1975, Malkiel 1959, Ransom 1979, Siewierska 1988). They take into consideration some specific linguistic structures like noun phrases, dative movement and coordinate idioms. Following Cooper and Ross, an extraordinary survey has been studied by Allan (1987) who identifies a set of hierarchies as determinants of noun phrase orderings. Allan classifies the linearity hierarchies suggested by various linguists into three groups: formal hierarchies, dominance hierarchies, and familiarity hierarchies. The formal hierarchies encompass matters of length and internal syntactic complexity. The dominance hierarchies cover factors connected with perceptions of natural salience as reflected in the way humans experience the world. Finally, the familiarity hierarchies deal with the speaker's individual interests as manifested in discourse via parameters such as topicality, givenness, definiteness and so forth (Kim 1995: 179). The list of hierarchies given below in (14) represents the major hierarchies in each of these three groups[①]:

(14) A. The Formal Hierarchies:

(a) structurally simpler > structurally complex

(b) short > long

B. The Dominance Hierarchies:

(a) The personal hierarchy:

1st p. > 2nd p. > 3rd p. human > higher animals > other organisms > inorganic matter > abstracts

(b) The semantic role hierarchy:

agent > patient > recipient > benefactive > instrumental > spatial > temporal

C. The Familiarity Hierarchies:

(a) more familiar > less familiar

(b) topic > comment

(c) given > new

(d) definite > indefinite

(e) referential > non-referential

Given these hierarchies, it is identified that the first two hierarchies are quite sensitive to word order phenomena at the sentence level, whereas the final one, the familiarity hierarchies, conforms to constraints on word order at the discourse level. Based on Allan's classification, Sierwierska (1988) offers an extensive discussion on each group of hierarchies. She notes that the factors mentioned in the linearity hierarchies are closely interrelated and linear precedence relations tend to be determined by several coinciding factors or features rather than an individual one.

It is seemingly seen that Allan's hierarchies serve to be a satisfactory explanation to

① In the list, the items to the left of " > " are understood as showing a preference to precede those on the right of " > ".

word order issues. The hierarchies establish criteria for the sequencing of linguistic elements in English. However, the previous studies in word order facts have shown that Allan's hierarchies are not flawless because the factors in the hierarchies can only explain the sequence of noun phrases at or above the sentence level. Indeed, word order variants can happen in various grammatical scopes. The positions of verb phrases and adjectives, for example, can also be changed to meet semantic or pragmatic needs. Moreover, the hierarchies separately take noun phrases into consideration, whether dependent on the discourse context or not. It is believed that the arrangement or movement of one element can be influenced by other elements within inside the sentence. What we are searching for is an approach or principles that can overwhelmingly and considerably cover any types of constituents in grammatical scopes.

2.1.4. Cognitive accounts

Despite the prosperous achievements from the semantic field, word order study continues to be active in linguistic field. But the attention has greatly penetrated to an extensive linguistic elements even including the orders of modifying clauses, cataphoric relation, subject pronouns (de Schutter 1987, Downing and Noonan 1995) etc. Though few linguists have put efforts into investigating cognitive accounts of the order of linguistic elements, the observations by some scholars have caused a stir in the process of positioning word order within the fields of psychology and linguistics. One of the representatives in these areas is Johnson-Llaird (1983).

Diehl (1975) ambitiously undertakes the explanation of not only the ordering of the three basic constituents, but also indirect objects and oblique noun phrases. His investigation is conducted by proposing five major factors: ego-deictic iconicity, temporal iconicity, linkage iconicity, discourse structure and model strings. Diehl is the first to include cognitive factors in the explanation of word order facts. Though the basic approach that Diehl develops is both systematic and comprehensive, he is truly criticized by Tomlin (1986: 39) he elaborates that "all of the principles Diehl uses are not motivated well in his study. The primary difficulty is that little data is presented, and most of what is presented come from English." In other words, Diehl has presented a cognitive explanation, but his idea cannot be convincing from a typological point of view.

Next to be mentioned should be the efforts from Krupa (1982), who presents a very brief but elegant discussion of the order of the basic constituents. His explanation involves the interaction of three fundamental principles: sentence depth, the cognitive factor and the relative structural independence. What deserves to be highlighted is his cognitive principle which can well be called the natural iconicity of linguistic expression. Those elements that are ordered earlier in the sentence represent the earlier stages of the event described by the proposition. Though logical and creative, Krupa's account has been the target of numerous criticisms from functionalists because they claim that Krupa's three principles are quite imaginative and cannot be well motivated from either a cognitive or a cross-linguistic point of view.

A rough sketch of word order studies is of great significance because in the following sections, the literature on word order within coordinate idioms and prenominal modifiers will be discussed respectively and they will not be well understood without the background on word order study.

2.2. Previous studies on the order of coordinate idioms

The fact that the order of coordinate idioms remains unchanged continually renders us to think over: Why is the first word always prior to the second, but not vice versa? What is the principle in keeping such a word order? Nunberg et al (1994) offer an explanation of these idioms with one necessary feature which is conventionality:

Their meaning or use cannot be predicted, or at least entirely predicted, on the basis of knowledge of the independent conventions that determine the use of their constituents when they appear in isolation from one another. (p. 492)

Nowadays however, bulks of studies hold a widely acknowledged view that the order of coordinate idioms is in effect governed by certain rigorous and recurrent rules external to language and hence predictable. For instance Landsberg (1995: 223) insists that "such phenomena, sometimes also called 'linguistic freezes', are fixed in a non-arbitrary order, although of course not all freezes necessarily have to be iconic."

The earliest literature for the order of coordinate idioms comes from Malkiel (1959), who generalizes six forces which determine the sequence of coordinate idioms. He even gives a description of the interplay of the six forces, which is shown below:

(15) The six forces which determine the sequence of coordinate idioms given by Malkiel:

(a) chronological priority of A①

(b) priorities inherent in the structure of a society

(c) precedence of the stronger of two polarized traits②

(d) patterns of formal preferences③

(e) precedence of A due to internal diffusion

(f) transmission of sequence through loan translation. (pp. 143 – 152)

① According to Malkiel (1959:143), the first force "does not mean the precedence of the referent of A over the referent of B in real-life situation, but the expansion, with passage of time, of a monomial (A) into a binomial (A + 1 + B)".

② Malkiel (1959:148) mentions that this force refers to "a tendency for one of the two contrastive features to assume the status of a basic or positive trait and for its opposite to signal the lack of that trait".

③ Malkiel (1959:149) claimed that this force refers to "the purely formal preference of numerous speech communities for a certain configuration of the binomials, describable by the qualitative and quantitative distribution of sounds, accentual and tonal schemas, total lengths of segments, and the like".

Malkiel's forces have more or less touched on the correlation between linguistic forms and the experience in the real world, namely forces (a), (b) and (e). Unfortunately, he just mingles them with those factors that are unnaturally generated and fails to single them out. He even does not conduct deeper attempts to providing explanations for his generalizations.

Cooper and Ross (1975) notice some cases in which the phonological and semantic constraints interact systematically with each other. They also propose a common appeal to the order of coordinate idioms based on the self-evident semantic principle, the so-called "Me First" principle: First conjuncts refer to those factors which describe the prototypical speaker (1975: 67).

Many Chinese scholars (Chen and Yu 1979, E 2001) also find that phonology, in particular four tones in Chinese, determines the order of Chinese coordinate idioms, whereas Zhang (1980) holds that the only way to understanding the order of Chinese coordinate idioms is by investigating their semantic and grammatical rules. The reason that certain Chinese researchers merely restrict their studies to the scope of phonological factors rather than that of semantic factors is that Chinese is exemplified as the only language which is typical of its four tones. This leads them to the belief that the order of coordinate idioms is greatly influenced by phonology. In recent years, many linguists (Cheng and Zhang 1989, Zhang 1996, Zu 2002) insist that the two factors should be incorporated to yield the order of coordinate idioms.

These attempts to explain the order of coordinate idioms conducted by researchers from both English and Chinese are based on a significant description of the linguistic forms dependant on phonological and semantic constraints. Compared with the generative grammarians, they have made a great step forward to focus on the meaning rather than the form. However, their isolating meaning from form does not enable them to provide a plausible interpretation to formulate rules because they cast attention to intra-linguistic factors and overlook many extra-linguistic oncs, which leave it deficient in accounting for the linguistic phenomena. We have noted the cases that linguistic form which is subsequently encoded by human conceptual experience is in reality closely related to its meaning. It leads to the later credence that an iconic function can be identified to explain either the inner properties of the fixed expressions (e. g. when a linguistic form mimes a form of nature as in the expressions "land and sea" or "cat and mouse") or the fixed orders determined by the social context of occurrence (e. g. the object signified is not physically present but may be recovered in the social setting, as in the constituents "yes or no", "coffee and cake"). In doing so, the form is iconically related to the meaning in the course of determining the sequential order of the coordinate idioms.

With the advent of cognitive theories, a great number of studies have announced that the structure of coordinate idioms as a part of language system is basically represented by the structure of human concepts. Thus the processes in which these coordinate idioms are ordered are from the cognitive abilities that human beings use outside the domain of language and hence it is predictable. For this reason many scholars turn to biology or psychology to seek for the answer. The most influential one is Edmondson (1985: 66) who holds that the first conjunct of a coordinate idiom "tends to be the unmarked of prototypical element".

Among other theories explaining the order of coordinate idioms, cognitive psychological linguists cannot be ignored. For instance, Allott (1995) claims that, evolutionarily speaking, language is constructed on the basis of an already existing neural motor system:

> The motor system, prior to the development of language, was built up from a limited number of primitive elements — units of action — that could be formed into more extended motor programs. This would allow one to derive the processes of word formation and syntactic rules for constructing

word sequences from the neural rules governing the union of motor elements into simple and motor complex actions [...] (pp. 310 – 311)

Other claim arises from the biological process behind language. Dotter (1995) provides this multidimensional assumption:

The structure of the organism and necessities of learning and communicating, as well as economic principles (which overlap evolution, learning, and communication), lead to a structuring/systemization of the coding material. (p. 47)

From both the fixed expression perspective and the idea that motor programs themselves could help to define syntax, we are faced with the idea that human conceptual or perceptual structures in the experiential world can contribute to the linear arrangement of coordinate idioms (Landsberg 1995). According to Landsberg, humanity's gestalt perception itself is revealed in coordinate idioms. For instance, the perception of oneself as the center of all things reveals itself in a tendency to see the zero-point of reference in an utterance to be where we are at, in both time and space. Thus, we say "*in and out*" rather than "*out and in*", "*here and there*" rather than "*there and here*". This principle combined with a masculine prominence in world view could contribute to such frozen orderings such as "*father and mother*", "*husband and wife*" and "*boys and girls*", although there truly exist counter-examples like the coordinate idiom "*bride and groom*".

In sum, modern linguists do not deny the crucial role which iconicity plays in the ordering of coordinate idioms. However, the analysis from some scholars probes deeply into the psychological factors, such as the neural system, biological, cognitive and psychological activities. These researchers' explanations mainly focus on the relation between the human cognitive system and language processing in general. Few, probably except for Landsberg, feel safe to specify their cognitive linguistic approach into the ordering of coordinate idioms. For instance, cognitive psychology, proposed by Allott (1995) as the theoretical basis of linguistic knowledge, can explicitly explain the order of coordinate idioms but he only implicitly touches on the issue of coordinate idioms.

The present study, however, will find adequate evidence from coordinate idioms to identify a conceptual constraint determined by conceptual processing construction in human beings which can be seen in the instances like "*rise and fall*", "*cause and effect*" and "*pain and gain*" and an information-processing constraint is seen in the examples that are culturally-determined and preferred in linguistic forms such as "*left and right*" and "*positive or negative*". The intention is to prove that the fixed order of coordinate idioms can also be formulated and accounted for based on human conceptual structure.

Unlike the traditional comparative studies that are carried out by finding their similarities and differences from their linguistic outward forms (Zhang and Zhang 1996, Li 2001), the recent studies begin to consider the semantic factors affecting the order of coordinate idioms. However, their efforts (Wang 2002, Cao 2004, Wang 2002) are merely given to the generalization of the semantic relations, overlooking the cognitive abilities possessed by language users. Thus their failure to provide an accurate explanation of the problem makes their studies bear some limitations.

Wen (2001) and Lu (2002) are the earliest scholars to apply iconicity to the exploration to the orders of both English and Chinese coordinate idioms. They say that the order is mainly governed by four principles: iconic sequence, closeness to the speaker, proximity iconicity, and conventional or cultural iconicity. In effect their explanations are less convincing because few data are included to illustrate their theoretic explanation, as what Xie (2005) has commented that some of the data cannot be attributed to the category of coordinate idioms at all. Regarding these drawbacks, the present study attempts to collect substantial and appropriate data from both English and Chinese first-hand sources to gain support for the adoption of the iconic factors in linguistic structure of coordinate idioms. The iconic factor is chosen because of its widespread explanatory power in the structures of coordinate idioms. At the same time, the characteristics of iconicity can allow to relate conceptual constraints to those phonological and semantic constraints investigated before (e. g. monosyllable preceding disyllable related to the simpler before more complex rule, etc.). In other words, the employment of iconicity principles can possibly open up a more comprehensive research consideration into the ordering of coordinate idioms.

2. 3. Previous studies on the order of prenominal modifiers within a noun phrase

Modifiers within English noun phrases include both prenominal modifiers and post-nominal modifiers. However, a majority of languages in the world have a relatively larger proportion of prenominal modifiers than that of post-nominal modifiers. Consequently, this study mainly focuses on the ordering of prenominal modifiers within a noun phrase.

The previous studies of the prenominal modifier orderings have been conducted from at least three approaches: syntactic, semantic and cognitive perspectives. After the first study from syntactic perspective conducted by Chomsky (1973), who claims that the study is of no value because prenominal modifiers are merely optional constituents, Vendler (1968) regards the ordering of prenominal modifiers as a syntactic feature irrelevant to semantics. Yet others like Brown and Miller (1991) and van Valin and Lapolla (2002) keep on with their semantic approach and observe the unmarked order of the nominal construction in English: Determiner > Numeral > Adjective > Noun. Though their findings open a door for modifier research, their insightful contributions cannot abandon the pursuit of formal analysis.

Other scholars propose a functional perspective by stating that the relative ordering of premodifying adjectives in English is a monotonic function of the estimated effort involved in processing each adjective in the sequence. The simplest hypothesis derivable from such processing considerations is that the adjective which conveys the least information should be preferred in initial position, and the adjective with the highest Communicative Dynamics value should be placed closest in distance to the head noun. They focus on explanatory principles out of communicative system which is regarded as external to language, rather than on the structure of languages related to the human conceptual or experiential structure. Thus it is usually hard to effectively parallel their Communicative Dynamics value with the appropriate ordering when adjectives sharing the similar attributes co-exist in a single noun phrase. Such as in the phrase "*a beautiful big tall American woman*", if we consider that the adjective "*beautiful*" conveys the most important information in the communicative context, can we possibly say the phrase in this way: "*a big tall American beautiful woman*"?

Those who made the greatest contributions to this area are English semantic linguists like Goyvaerts (1968), Hetzron (1978), Quirk et al (1985), Bache (1978) and Dixon (1982). Their exhaustive analyses based on their manually-built small corpora help present various tendencies, such as the facts that underivable adjectives often precede derivable adjectives, and shorter modifiers precede longer ones. Given the difficulty of adequately describing all factors that influence the order of prenominal modifiers, much of earlier work is based on placing the prenominal modifiers into broad semantic classes, and specifying an order among these classes. Usually more than ten classes have been proposed, with some of them further broken down into subclasses.

Though not all these studies agree on the details, they demonstrate that there is fairly rigid regularity in the ordering of adjectives when they function as premodifiers, among whom Goyvaerts (1968: 27) proposes the order of "quality > size/length/shape > old/new/young > color > nationality > style > gerund > denominal". Quirk et al (1985) argue for a subjective-objective gradience determining adjective order by stating that,

> One is tempted to suggest one principle accounting not only for all general adjectives but all premodifiers: a subjective/objective polarity. That is, modifiers relating to properties which are (relative) inherent in the head of the noun phrase, visually observable, objectively recognizable or assessable, will tend to be placed nearer to the head and be preceded by modifiers concerned with what is relatively a matter of opinion, imposed on the head by the observer, not visually observed and only subjectively accessible. (p. 1341)

Some researchers in the proceeding studies investigate adjective ordering from the typological perspective (Dixon 1982, Frawley 1992). Frawley (1992), for cxample, observes that English, German, Hungarian, Polish, Turkish, Hindi, Persian, Indonesian, and Basque all order value before size and both the value and size before color.

In his analysis of inter-language class correspondences, Dixon (1982: 30) identifies seven subclasses of adjectives, arguing that "each semantic type has, in particular language, its own particular norm and extensional grammatical properties", the latter also including its position in a string of adjectives. Take a look at Table 1 for an overview.

Table 1: Dixon's semantic classes and their hypothesized order

SEQUENCE CODE	7	6	5	4	3	2	1
SEMANTIC CLASS	Value	Dimension	Physical Property	Speed	Human Propensity	Age	Color

续表

SEQUENCE CODE	7	6	5	4	3	2	1
DIXON'S EXAMPLES	*good*, *bad*	*big*, *long*	*hard*, *sweet*	*quick*, *slow*	*happy*, *kind*	*new*, *young*	*red*, *white*

At the same time, Chinese grammarians (Gu 1986, Zhang 1998, and among others) carry out the classification of prenominal modifiers on both English and Chinese languages in light of semantic properties. Zhang (1998) detailedly classifies the order of prenominal adjectives in English as "general descriptive adjectives > size/length/height > shape > age > color > nationality/ provenance/ origin > material > type".

These heuristic classifications surely provide a comprehensive description of the semantic domains depending on the semantic features of different prenominal modifiers. However, their approach does not consider the constraints from the central constituent of the whole noun phrase. That is, former research assumes that the ordering of prenominal modifiers has nothing to do with the head noun. However, is that true that the ordering of prenominal modifiers, as elements dependent on the head noun, is not closely related to the semantic properties of the head noun? They fail to explain why, when some modifiers do not fall into the corresponding semantic category, the sentence is still grammatical. A good case in point is the English pair examples "*dirty British books*" and "*British dirty books*". When the premodifier "*dirty*" moves before and after "*British*", the meanings of the two phrases totally change. However, the classification-based approach can easily lure people to a blind credence to the ungrammaticality of the phrase "*British dirty books*".

Fischer (2001) might be the first to make an investigation into the position of the adjectives in (old) English serving as modifiers from an iconic perspective. She observes,

"Adjective position in Old English is iconically motivated in that prenominal adjectives, when they are weak and definite, convey given information; they behave typically like attributive adjectives which are closer to the nominal pole of the adjective cline, and they are therefore an inseparable part of the head: together with the noun phrase they form the "theme" of the utterance (pp. 251 - 276)."

Though she touches on the properties of prenominal modifiers, the efforts in the article are mostly trying to distinguish the positions of prenominal and post-nominal modifiers, but not to identify the specific sequential order among prenominal modifiers.

Owing to the unsatisfactory solutions to the problem, it is inevitable to continue for a cogent interpretation. In their *An Introduction to Cognitive Linguistics*, Ungerer and Schmid (1996) offer an account of ordering prenominal modifiers in light of Haiman's distance principle of iconicity. The following examples are given to illustrate their opinions, which is shown in (16).

(16) a. the famous delicious Italian pepperoni pizza

b. * the Italian delicious famous pepperoni pizza

c. * the famous pepperoni delicious Italian? pizza

d. * the pepperoni delicious famous Italian pizza (Urgerer and Schmid 1996: 253)

Recall that in distance principle the linguistic elements that are semantically and conceptually related to each other should be placed close together. In the example (16), four adjectives precede the head noun "*pizza*". However the ordering of these modifiers is fixed, but not arbitrary, as indicated by the grammaticality contrast between (a) and (b-d). Urgerer and Schmid (1996: 253 - 254) claim that the four modifiers have different degrees of semantic and conceptual relationship with the head noun. The meaning of the modifier "*pepperoni*" contains an inherent property of this kind of pizza. Since it is conceptually closest to the head noun "*pizza*", it precedes the head noun immediately; the modifier "*Italian*", which represents the origin of the pizza, is semantically less closely related to the noun than the modifier "*pepperoni*", but less distant than the other two modifiers "*famous*" and "*delicious*" because the adjective "*delicious*" tends to denote a person's subjective opinion towards an entity, similarly the adjective modifier "*famous*" revealing one's emotional evaluation towards an entity perceived by people in the world. They are mentally, however loosely related to the head noun, and therefore they take the furthest positions within an English noun phrase. These differences in conceptual relationships to the head noun shown in adjectives are directly reflected in their orders within a noun phrase which is later summarized as "the closer the adjectives are conceptually related to the head noun, the closer the positions they take in relation to the head noun".

The viewpoint from Urgerer and Schmid receives great attentions and few challenges. The problem, however, remains that they fail to explicitly generalize the semantic properties of those adjectives to explain why they need to be close to the head noun. That is, they do not provide evidential explanation to show what kinds of adjectives are conceptually related to the head noun, or what linguistic or semantic criteria can distinguish the distance between the head noun and its modifiers. Take the phrase "*a bamboo fishing pole*" for example. According to Urgerer and Schmid, because the modifier "*Bamboo*", which is indicating the material of the pole, designates the inherent property of the head noun, it needs to be closer to the head noun in linguistic structure concerning about their conceptual closeness. Furthermore, the modifier "*bamboo*" precedes the other modifier "*fishing*", and is placed in a relatively distant position from the head noun because the modifier "*fishing*" describes the "function" property of the head noun which is conceptually considered very close from the center of the phrase, consequently nearer in semantic construal.

Haiman (1985a: 102) proposes the standpoint of conceptual closeness in 1985, which is believed to be in accordance with the "distance principle" given in his proceeding articles. It holds that the linearity of a linguistic structure is iconically correspondent with the distance of conceptual expression between entities revealed in real world. It is later on developed into the distance principle within the iconicity theory, which says that the distance shown between linguistic elements matches with the distance that is conceptually represented among things. It accounts for the idea given by Slobin who announces that "what belongs together mentally is placed close together syntactically (Slobin 1997: 314)." The Distance Principle by Haiman (1985a:106 – 107) can be described as follows:

(17) Two ideas are conceptually close to the extent that they

a. share semantic features, properties or parts;

b. affect each other;

c. are factually inseparable;

d. are perceived as a unit, whether factually inseparable or not.

Haiman further gives the following illustration to decrease the linguistic distance between two linguistic elements X and Y.

(18) a. X# A# B# Y

b. X# A# Y

c. X + A# Y

d. X# Y

e. X + Y

f. Z① [= fusion of X and Y into a single form] (Haiman 1985a: 105, ex. 88)

---

① According to Haiman (1985a:105), the illustration in (18f) is the synthesis of the morphemes X and Y into a single morph, which may be, but is not necessarily identical with either linguistic element X or element Y.

In the scale given in (18), the symbol "#" represents the word boundary, while the symbol " + " represents the morpheme boundary. The scales from (18a) to (18f) indicate a gradually strengthening degree of the closeness among elements. Accordingly, many linguistic phenomena can be resided in to evince the feasibility of the iconic principle of conceptual closeness. Take the phrases (19) and (20) for examples:

(19) a. lighthouse keeper

b. light housekeeper

(20) a. a paper boy/ a paperboy

b. a black mail/ a blackmail

Judging from the scale in (18) given by Haiman, the noun phrase "h*ouse keeper*" in example (19a) and the noun form "*housekeeper*" in example (19b) belong to different scales in that there is a word boundary symbol "#" between the nominal word "*house*" and the nominal word "*keeper*" in (19a), thus the two words are separated from each other in form. On the contrary, the lack of word boundary leads us to believe that they actually form into a compound word with a single morpheme boundary in the example (19b) though they can be regarded as two isolated words. Consequently, the meanings denoted in the two examples are not identical.

Although each of the two examples in (20a) and (20b) consists of two identical words "*paper*" "and" "*boy*", "*black*" and "*mail*", the two words that are put in isolation cause semantic differences from those that are merged in the forms of compound words, if it is the case that the linguistic distance can mirror conceptual distance and reveal semantic distinctions. Intuitively, a plausible explanation could be that in example (20a), the noun phrase "*a paper boy*" refers to a boy made of paper, while the noun phrase "*a paperboy*" means a boy whose job is to deliver the newspapers. Following the semantic distinction investigation of the examples in (20a), the word forms shown in example (20b) can also be understood and illustrated to support the fact that linguistic distance corresponds to the conceptual distance.

Moving back to the order arrangement of prenominal modifiers, the distance between prenominal modifiers and the head noun needs to be taken into consideration if Haiman's Conceptual Closeness Principle has to be followed. Therefore, it comes the hypothesis that if the linguistic distance between the prenominal modifier and the head noun is symbolized as the representative distance between X and Y. The distance between a modifier and the head within a noun phrase is determined by whether or not there is a third morpheme linking the two elements in the construction, and what is the type of boundary between the two elements: morpheme boundary or word boundary. For instance, the symbolic distance among the indefinite article "*a*" and the head noun "*ball*" within the noun phrase "*a big red ball*", should be represented as "X# A# B# Y"; among which symbol Y represents the head noun; the symbol "#" embodies the different linguistic distances among the other linguistic elements with the head noun Y. Under the guidance that the differences in linguistic distance mirror the differences in the conceptual distance, the phrase can be interpreted such as that the conceptual distance between the adjectival modifier "*big*" and the head noun "*ball*" is greater than that between the adjectival modifier "*red*" and the head "*ball*".

On account of the above-mentioned fact, a motivated hypothesis can be predicted for the order of prenominal modifiers, saying that in the process of ordering prenominal modifiers, the closer position of the modifiers to the head noun can be indicated by the closer concepts between the two elements, while the linguistic position distant from the head will be indicated by the possibility that the two elements do not have an intimate conceptual relation. Illustrations are needed to prove whether this hypothesis can be confirmed.

(21) a. my three nice little white wooden dolls

b. a beautiful big red ball

According to the hypothesis that the closest the modifier is linguistically to the head, the closest it is conceptually to the head, an analysis into example (21a) goes like this: in English, the adjective modifier "*wooden*" indicates the main character of the entity "*doll*", which can deeply influence the state of the head noun "*doll*". That is, if the "*wooden*" feature as substances is transformed, the physical state of the thing will change correspondently. Owing to their interactive affection, the adjective "*wooden*" is placed the closest to the head in the linguistic symbolization. Different from the adjective "*wooden*", the modifiers "*little*" and "*white*" all describe the superficial features of the entity. They linguistically stay further from the head noun, compared to the adjective modifier "*wooden*". But compared with the modifier "*little*", the adjective "*white*" designated the color of a physical substance is inclined to stay conceptually closer than the modifier "*little*" because it usually indicates the size of the thing and is always considered as dynamic within attribute-categorization. Thus the adjective "*white*" is placed closer to the head than that "*little*". Obviously, both of the adjectival modifiers cannot strongly affect the state of the head. In other words, the change of color or size cannot change the state of the head. Thus they are positioned relatively farther than the modifier "*wooden*" to the head noun. The adjective "*nice*" can never show the static character of an entity; instead it implies the personal opinion from the observer and contains subjectivity feature to certain extent. It is placed quite distant from the head compared to the other three adjectives because it is not conceptually inseparable from the head. Generally speaking, numerals carry the sense of selection from certain objects so they are conceptually closer and thus placed closer to the head than possession modifiers, but further than attributes. In a word, these illustrations can account for their ordering in the direction of conceptual distance iconicity. However, this is by far an explicit illustration because up to now an objective criterion is not yet to be reached to assess which adjective is conceptually close to or distant from the head. Naturally, the task in the present study is to conduct investigation into what semantic features or properties prenominal modifiers can have to make them closer to the head noun.

The findings show that it is notoriously difficult to come to a generalization for the explanation of ordering the adjectives within a noun phrase. The reason is that it is by far easy to follow a powerful theoretical framework to include all data used in the natural language occurrences. Despite of all these, the present research intends not to argue against the standpoint raised by previous scholars, instead to implement their viewpoint will be done by adding the analysis of the semantic properties of the head noun to the semantic observation on its modifiers and provide the principles of iconicity as theoretical evidene, to explain the relations between the distance among linguistic elements and their conceptual structure closeness.

2.4. Discussion and summary

To conclude the chapter, it is found that the previous investigation to word order phenomenon mainly dwells itself on the scope of typological and functional fields. The overextension of the cross-linguistic database and the overstatement of communicative purposes hinder researchers to notice the inner match between language and human cognitive capacities, leading their findings only to be linguistic descriptions of word order variations. In other words, the studies in the literature fail to adhere to the research rationale that the majority of linguistic structures correspond to human physical and conceptual structures which are depicted in the experienced world, which is believed to be the essence in the field of cognitive linguistics. Therefore, the present study believes that as one of the representative proposals of the cognitive theory, Haiman's iconicity principles are of significance in solving the puzzles at issue.

The previous studies on the ordering of coordinate idioms (Cooper and Ross 1975,

Malkiel 1959, Cheng and Zhang 1989, Zhang 1996, Zu 2002) are in large part confined to phonological and semantic constraints or the interactions with one another, and are characterized a significant description of the linguistic forms based on the two constraints mentioned above. However, another look reveals that the aspect of constraints cannot truly provide a plausible interpretation to the semantically relevant ordering of the coordinate idioms because they mainly focus on the language itself, overlooking the relation between linguistic structure and human conceptual structure. A close observation into data could verify the fact that the iconic function is able to be applied to interpret either the ordering constraints of the fixed expressions when they are miming the features of the entities in the real world, or the rules of the fixed orders determined by the social setting. In doing so, the idea that researchers looking into the fixed orders of coordinate idioms can seek for their interpretations from language users' conceptual system is workable.

As far as the ordering of prenominal modifiers is concerned, a great number of contributions come from semantic linguists. Though their classifications of prenominal modifiers are appropriate and reasonable, they ignore the fact that the modifiers are only constituents parasitic to the head noun. In effect, if only the semantic properties of the head noun are taken into consideration, the distance between modifier and the head would naturally be understood and interpreted through the conceptual distance in human minds.

Bearing these in mind, the present study assumes that human language is a human evolutionary product paralleled by relations among concepts or elements of discourse. In the meantime, iconicity, as the representative of cognitive linguistics, lays its point of contact on the level of human conceptual processing towards the interaction among the entities in the physical world to provide explanatory forces on the close relation between the form and meaning of languages. Thus it is reasonably appealed to the discussion of word order within noun phrases and the ordering of coordinate idioms as well. It has also been found that the iconic choices of linguistic structures have ranged through various language levels but touched little at the phrasal level. Thus the present thesis assumes that iconicity principles can help to solve the problem at issue. The following chapter will present a review of how iconicity theory takes shape and illustrate the three principles of iconicity and how they are employed in the linguistic field.

CHAPTER THREE
THEORETICAL FRAMEWORK: ICONICITY AND ICONICITY PRINCIPLES

Different from arbitrariness, which means no connection between linguistic form and the conceptual processing of the entities in real world, iconicity is a study of the similarity or the natural relationship between linguistic structure and conceptual structure that linguistic symbols represent. Iconicity, according to the explanation of Croft (2000: 164), is a type of external motivation for linguistic structure. The debating issue whether human language is constructed in terms of arbitrariness or iconicity, evoked fervent discussions as early as the dawn of scientific linguistic thoughts, and never seems to cease. Although both sides tend to accept that both arbitrariness and non-arbitrariness exist in language, neither has won the argument against the other.

Despite the fact that the linguistic study performed by earlier scholars has emphasized the "arbitrariness" and "conventionality" of linguistic structures, there are aspects of language that suggest a certain iconicity — a structural similarity to the referents. Today the issue of iconicity has greatly and surprisingly influenced particular aspects of linguistics and maybe some other areas will shortly be influenced. It is apparent that the iconicity's history of struggles against arbitrariness witnesses the developmental history of iconicity.

Simon (1994: vii) names the two opposite patterns as Platonic Paradigm① and Aristotelian-Saussurean Paradigm. ② It is seemingly a good solution to the distinction between arbitrariness and iconicity. However, he proposes to explain the debate between arbitrariness and/or iconicity within a synchronic, as opposed to a diachronic perspective. For ease of discussion, unlike Simon, the diachronic viewpoint is highlighted to divide the argumentative history between arbitrariness and/or iconicity into three stages. Moreover, the fact noted by Peirce should be clearly stated to prove that the distinction between arbitrariness and/or iconicity is not a sharp one, but rather a matter of degree. As he has said that presumably a sign which resembles its object with respect to a thousand details is more iconic than one which resembles it in only a hundred (Haiman 1985a: 10). Grounded on his opinion, the credence which is held in this book is that every sign has to be iconic of the concept it represents. It simply is to what degree the sign is iconized or de-iconized.

This chapter mainly reviews the argumentative history of how the debate is rooted from the ancient Greek, illuminated by Saussure and evolved by Peirce. From time to time their precedence or predominance is compared until it is finally clear how iconicity is taken up again in this continuation of debate. After that, the currently pervasive principles of iconicity are illustrated with representative instances.

3. 1. Arbitrariness versus Iconicity

What are followed in the present chapter are the opposing arguments that are ex-

---

① Platonic Paradigm means language and reality must resemble each other to some extent if we want to be able to speak of reality without necessarily referring to it directly (Simon 1994: vii).

② Aristotelian-Saussurean Paradigm claims that language and reality are quite independent of, and do not resemble, each other; this is claimed to be so for reasons of economy and "handiness", since no language could be used if not arbitrarily structured (Simon 1994: vii).

posed to the historical viewpoint so that it will be clearer to demonstrate that linguistic structures are iconic.

3.1.1. Two theories at a deadlock (from ancient Greece to late in the 19th century)

When ancient Greek Philosophers argue about the relationship between names and things, there raises the difference of Naturalists and Conventionists, or Realism and Nomomalism. The essence of the argument is the very question of arbitrariness and/or iconicity.

In his *Cratylus*①, Plato (1926), as the representative of the Naturalists, maintains that names can reveal the essence of things, and there is natural connection between names and things. Leibniz (1981: 333) and Humboldt (Yao 1997: 72) agree upon it by stating that languages are the best mirror of the human mind, which implies that there exists a connection between the form and the content of language. Opposite to it, Aristotle, who holds the view of Conventionists/Nomomalism, voices that "there can be no natural connection between the sound of any language and the thing signified (Chandler 2002: 26)." His followers are Locke (1994) and Whitney (1869) both of whom have conducted researches to argue for the arbitrary relationship between a sound pattern and a concept.

The debate seems to be an unending war where neither is demolished until the early 20th century which turns to be a relatively silent period. This happens because of the general acceptance of Saussure's notion which assumes that language sign is a radically arbitrary entity and the consequent negative attitude towards the material constraints on language.

---

① According to Masako (1998:95 – 123), in Plato's dialogue *Cratylus* reminds us of the debate whether the relationship of form and content in language in set *Physei* (by nature) or *nomöi*, *ethei* (by agreement and convention)

3.1.2. The stage of Saussure's arbitrariness (from early the 20th century to the 1960s)

In the early 20th century,[①] Saussure stakes out the arbitrary relationship between the signifier and the signified of language in his posthumously-published classical work *Course in general Linguistics*. He upholds that language is an arbitrary symbolic vocal system because there is no intrinsic tie between the signifier and the signified (1983: 67–70). Saussure stresses the arbitrariness as the fundamental principle of semiology. Since then, the structural theory has come to exert a pervasive and enduring influence well into the contemporary period. Many linguists (Meillet 1970, Sapir 2001, Hockett 1958, Bloomfield 2002, Chomsky 1972) have unchangeably stuck to the idea of arbitrariness.

For generations, arbitrariness has been a dogma of linguistics. However, such a view has come under increasing fire. With the thriving development of diversified approaches to linguistic study, many scholars express their dissatisfactions and disagreements. They underline that there are some aspects in which linguistic representations are exactly what they seem to be in the physical or real world. The relevant study of iconicity is called for by those scholars for full attention.

It is Peirce who first originates the notion of iconicity as a semiotic principle. He regards language as a complex sign named diagram, representing a complex concept (Haiman 1985a: 9). He focuses on the relation between the sign and the object it re-

① The early 20th century is considered as the age of Ferdinand de Saussure who is called the founder of modern linguistics. He founded structuralism and led linguistics study towards a systematic direction.

presents and he proposes three types of signs — icon, index and symbol,① in which the sign can be employed to stand for its object. Peirce further divides icon into three hypoicons:② image, diagram and metaphor. Peirce's sign theory opens up a fresh perspective of observing linguistic aspects. His attempts have maximally reflected the designated trend of the structure of grammars. Nevertheless, no matter how convincing his idea is, Peirce does not receive enough attention because of Saussure's great influence at that time.

3.1.3. The stage of post-Saussure's opposition to arbitrariness (from the 1960s to the present)

In the 1960s, linguists seem to raise their awareness that language in a large portion can be motivated. The first challenge comes from Jakobson, who, in his essay *Quest for the Essence of Language* (1971a: 345 – 59), expresses the approval of several linguists' opposing views to the arbitrary nature of language.

In the meantime, both functional linguists (Halliday 2000) and cognitive linguists (Heine 1997; Lakoff and Johnson 1980; Haiman 1983, 1985a, 1985b; Langacker 1987a, 1987b) believe that the relation between meaning and form is iconic rather than arbitrary. The account from cognitive linguists is very convincing because they start to

① According to Peirce, an icon is a sign which refers to the object that it denotes merely by virtue of characters of its own. And the sign possesses these characters whether any such object actually exists or not (e. g. a lead-pencil streak as representing a geometrical line); an index is a sign which refers to the object that it denotes by virtue of being really affected by that object (e. g. signs of smoke to indicate fire, signs of skeleton to indicate danger); a symbol is a sign which refers to the object that it denoted by virtue of a law, usually an association of general ideas, which operates to cause the symbol to be interpreted as referring to that object. Linguistic signs which are non-motivated belong to symbols.

② A hypoicon is a sign that is only similar to its object, and it shares only some features with its object. It involves "not only iconicity, but also to a great extent indexical or symbolic properties (Bouissac 1998:293)."

take language meaning as an embodied phenomenon, coming out of the interaction between man and reality, and at last come to a universal conclusion that language form or structure is to a considerable extent a reflection of the concept or conceptual structure it represents.

Because of the prospect of the opinion that language is a mapping of the knowledge of the world, the acceptance of iconicity fosters a better understanding of the relationship between language and nature or reality. The idea that linguistic form and meaning are highly motivated even causes an expansion of the research scope into fields of linguistic philosophy, cognitive psychology, cognitive linguistics, second language acquisition and foreign language teaching. Simone (1994) bravely predicts that the study of iconicity will not only invite a reconsideration of the nature of language but also change the cause of linguistic research.

Haiman (1980, 1983, 1985a, 1985b) characterizes iconicity as a set of "signs whose meaning in some crucial way resembles their form" (1985a: 109). Via substantial data, he demonstrates that diagrammatic iconicity is pervasively present in language, especially at the level of syntax. Haiman (1985a: 10) notices that "the 'words' of the language are themselves symbolic: but their 'grammar' is diagrammatically iconic." In most cases, icons in language are referred to as Peirce's iconic diagram: "in the syntax of every language, there are logic icons of the kind that are aided by conventional rules (1985a: 106)." Haiman (1983, 1985a) sees diagrammatic iconicity as resulting from the interplay of two factors: isomorphism① and motivation. ②

By isomorphism, it refers to one-to-one correspondence between form and meaning. Haiman means that every point in language corresponds to some points in the reality depicted (1985a: 11) or syntactic components correspond to the components of conceptual structures. Isomorphism is stated in uncompromising fashion by Bolinger (1977: x): "the natural condition of language is to preserve one form for one meaning, and one meaning for one form". The one-to-one correspondence can be illustrated by the examples as follows:

(22) a. Jill is *fussy*.

b. Jill is *a fussy budget*. (Bolinger 1981: 79)

(23) a. The dog *chewed* the bone.

b. The dog *chewed on* the bone. (Croft and Cruse 2004: 14)

As to the relation of iconicity to isomorphism, Givón (1985: 188) assumes that "a reasonable sense of iconicity must presuppose the notion of isomorphism so that an iconic code is an isomorphically constructed code".

Motivation in linguistics is intuitively defined as a perceived similarity between the structure of a diagram and the structure of the concepts that it represents (Haiman 1985a: 71). There is a correspondence between the relation within syntactic compo-

① Isomorphism (Haiman 1985:21) is explained as "the natural condition of language is to preserve one form for one meaning, and one meaning for one form, whether this be a single word or a grammatical construction [...] violation of isomorphism are: many-to-one, one-to-many, one-to-zero, and zero-to-one relations between points in the diagram and points in reality."

② Motivation as a linguistic term was introduced by Saussure (1983:181) to describe compound or complex signs like the French word *dix-neuf* (nineteen). Saussure's concept of motivation is identical with Peirce's notion of diagrammatic icon. Haiman (1985a:377) defines motivation as a perceived similarity between the structure of language and the structure of the concepts that it represents. In Kortman (1999:377), motivation means that parts in linguistic structure and parts in cognitive system correspond to each other.

nents and that within empirical structural components (Haiman 1980: 515 – 516). It refers to a correspondence between our perception of the world and our representation of this perception (Haiman 1980: 516). Newmeyer (1998b: 114) maintains that the relations among linguistic structures are paralleled by conceptual structures. The essence of motivation is generalized by Simone (1994) as follows:

(24)(i) If you see similar or related forms, the differences between these forms reflect different meanings;

(ii) The linguistic distance between two expressions would be equivalent to the time interval between them;

(iii) Conceptual function is composed of such actions as perceptual, thinking, cognitive, persuasive and hypothetical etc. The differences can be shown depending on the behavioral immediacy. (p. 122)

The following examples can show the first implication of motivation, as given in (24i).

(25) a. *Call* me tonight.

b. Will you give me *a call* tonight?

c. I gave him *one call* last night.

d. I *called* him *once* last night. (Kim 2007: 224)

The meanings of all the above-mentioned examples have one thing in common: "*call somebody*". But they denote different meanings because of their differences in forms. In sentence (25a), the act of calling is the main purpose/command to request somebody to do something, while the indefinite article "a" in sentence (25b) signifies the frequency of performing the action of calling to be "at least one" call. On the contrary, both example (25c) and example (25d) imply "calling only one time", respectively designating the meaning of "one call" as seen in example (25c) and thc meaning of "called once" as is used in sentence (25d). The only difference between the two sentences is that they profile the different aspect of actions, with the act in sentence (25c) focusing on "an act of giving" and that in sentence (25d) on "the one time of doing". Moving on to the examples (26), (27) and (28) can help understand the second implication given in (24ii):

(26) a. Harry is *not happy*.

b. Harry is *unhappy*.

(27) a. He was *shot dead*.

b. He was *shot to death*.

(28) a. I *found* that the chair *was uncomfortable*.

b. I *found* the chair *ϕ uncomfortable*.

The information explicitly coded linguistically does not itself establish the precise connection apprehended by the speaker and hearer in using an expression. As it is shown, although the two sentences in examples (26a) and (26b) denote the negative meaning with two different forms of negation: negator "*not*" and the prefix "*un-*", the closeness of the prefix "*un-*" to the adjective "happy" in syntactic distance evokes stronger negative feeling than its correspondence in the negative form "*not*" which goes directly but separately to the head adjective "*happy*" in the sentence. The semantic differences in both sentence (27a) and sentence (27b) imply that the former contains the meaning that the act of shooting directly causes the death of the person, while the latter maintains that the victim meets with other sufferings besides the act of shooting before he finally dies.

In the instances (28a) and (28b), the English verb "*found*" can be followed by both *that*-clause and small clause, superficially based on the rigid English grammar rules, though, it is often doubtful whether grammar is inherently symbolic referring to the conceptual structures in the physical world. Visually observing, readers can identify the language distance differences from between the verb "*found*" and the adjective "uncomfortable" in *that*-clause to between them as an object and a complement. Cognitive explanation leads to that if the experiencer goes and tries the comfort ability of the chair by himself/herself, then the sentence (28b) is preferable. Suppose the experiencer just expresses his/her indirect feeling towards the chair or merely sees the chair but without trying it personally, sentence (28a) is more appropriate. For the last implication of motivation in (24iii), consider the following examples.

(29) a. I *think/consider* you *a kind man.*

b. I *know* you *to be a kind man.*

c. I *want* you *to be a kind man.*

d. I *wish that you would be a kind man.*

If the close conceptual distance is reflected in the linguistic form, a noun phrase is applied immediately after the direct object. Thus the semantic denotation in sentence (29a) can be the moment the subject "I" exerts his energies to perform the act of "considering" or "thinking", you is already a kind man. But for the sentence (29d), the verb "wish" just implies a desire from the subject "I". And the use of subjunctive mood indicates the less possibility of the accomplishment of the agent's acting of wishing. Syntactically, a clause is employed after the main verb and subjunctive mood is added to lengthen the distance between two concepts if it is the fact that the conceptual distance is reflected in the linguistic structure.

Haiman's work triggers off a bulk of follow-up discussions on linguistic iconicity, and makes this long-shelved phenomenon re-enter the public mind. The dedicated researchers include Bybee (1985), Nanny and Fischer (1999), Givón (1990, 1995), Greenberg (1963), Kortmann (1999), Newmeyer (1998b), Norrman (1999), Simone (1994), Traugott (1982, 1985), Ungerer and Schmid (1996), and among others.

Iconicity study has similarly long been the mainstream of linguistic topic in China until to the recent years. Tracing back to the ancient times, stress is laid on the issue whether the meaning of a linguistic sign is embodied most obviously in pictographs. To date, many Chinese linguists are devoted to applying the principles of iconicity to the linguistic phenomena like Xu (1988), Shen (1993), Wang (1998, 1999, 2000), Wen (1999, 2000), Tai (1985, 1995). For instance, Tai (1988: 18) pinpoints that Mandarin Chinese, regarded as a non-inflectional language, has many syntactic forms following the temporal sequence principle of the depicted events in the real world, which is one of the concerned iconicity principle in this study. In effect, an elaborate study of iconicity cannot neglect a good understanding of its three principles.

3.2. Three principles of Iconicity

Haiman (1985a, 1985b) discusses the iconic exploitation of conceptual linearity, symmetry and distance projecting on the linguistic forms. Of existing work along these lines, a considerable number of ways have been suggested by which linguistic structure can iconically reflect conceptual structure. For instance, Ungerer and Schmid (1996) classify the principles of sequencing, proximity and quantity to reflect the motivation of iconicity after Givón (1990, 1995) proposes four principles: quantity principle, proximity principle, sequential order principle and markedness principle. It can be seen that their understandings of iconicity between meaning and form are identical in general. What differs is the terminology they have applied. In this thesis, three terminologies for the principles will be elaborated: Distance/Proximity Principle, Quantity Principle and Sequential Order Principle.

3. 2. 1. Distance/Proximity Principle

By Distance/Proximity Principle, it means that the distance between physical structures of entities in man's concepts can be projected onto the distance of linguistic structures. In other words, in spatial configuration, the entities which conceptually belong together tend to adhere to each other in linguistic forms, the notion of which is by far a new one. As early as the year of 1932, Behaghel (1932: 4) is credited with the first explicit statement of this principle, followed by Jespersen (1949: 56), who proposes a principle of cohesion, indicating that "ideas that are closely connected tend to be placed together." After Bolinger (1975: 137) examines the principle in his introductory book "Aspect of Language", the same idea has been repeatedly and effectively "rediscovered" by Lambrecht (1984) and Haiman (1985a), who both embodily refer the principle to a considerably extensive body of data. One of the implications of this principle is also illustrated by Givón (1990).

(30) Entities that are closer together functionally, conceptually, or cognitively will be placed closer together at the code level, i. e. temporally or spatially. (p. 970)

To illustrate, the Principle is reflected in the word order variations of dative movement in English, as shown in (31):

(31) a. We gave Fido the bone.
　　b. We gave the bone to Fido. (Green 1974: 158)

To account for such meaning differences, Hwang (2004) applies the Distance Principle to grammar analysis by stating that "the closer the object in a sentence is to the verb that denotes the subject's action, the more direct the effect of the verb on the object is." The semantic differences between the two examples can be obviously shown after the additional clauses are given as follows:

(32) a. * We gave Fido the bone, but he didn't take it.

b. We gave the bone to Fido, but he didn't take it.

It is seen from the sentence (32a), the object "*Fido*" is right next to the verb "*gave*". Depending on the explanation of Distance Principle, if the linguistic elements are placed close to each other, its conceptual representation indicates that they are greatly affected by each other semantically. Thus we can conclude that the close linguistic distance between the object "Fido" and the main verb "gave" in the first conjunct indicates that the receiver "Fido" has been greatly affected by our act of giving the bone to the extent that Fido finally received the bone successfully. On the contrary, the meaning of the second conjunct within this sentence denies such a successful transference. The semantic contradiction between the former and the latter part of the example leads to the semantic discongruity in sentence (32a). However, the meaning reflected in the sentence (32b) is sharply opposite: in the first conjunct, the receiver "Fido" is made distant from the verb "gave". It shows that the conceptual contents denoted in the two words fail to have effect on each other since they are placed afar. Consequently, the assumption is that the act of giving the bone to the receiver "Fido" might fail to be a successful transference. Naturally it can be linguistically linked to the second conjunct as it is shown that the sentence (32b) is both syntactically and semantically acceptable.

In his study of iconicity in syntax, Haiman (1985a) points out a multitude of cases where grammatical distance and conceptual distance are correlated. For instance, lexical causatives (e. g. kill) tend to convey a more direct causation than periphrastic causatives (e. g. cause to die). Consider:

(33) a. John caused Bill to die by inadvertently buying him a ticket on a plane that ended up crashing.

b. John killed Bill by inadvertently buying him a ticket on a plane that ended up crashing.

The oddness of (33b) results from the fact that the stronger causative force that the English word "kill" contains can convey a more direct causation meaning than the periphrastic causative phrase "cause to die". Thus, when the causative chain of cause and result are prolonged in linguistic forms, their conceptual distance is more distant than when they are not.

Along the same lines, Haiman (1985a) suggests that in no language will the linguistic distance be greater in signaling inalienable possession than it is in alienable possession. Greenberg (1963) notes that where number and case morphemes are not fused, the former are almost always closer to the head than the latter and less likely to be expressed as independent words. Bybee (1985: 10) provides evidence to show that the more "relevant" a reflection is to a head, the closer it is likely to be to that head and the more likely it is to be bound to that head, where the relevance of an inflection is measured in terms of the degree to which it directly modifies the head. We posit that the modifiers of a head tending form a constituent with that head can be illustrated by the Distance Principle.

3.2.2. Quantity Principle

The scholar who pioneered this inspiring principle is Jakobson (1971a: 345 – 359), and he claims that greatness of meaning in quantity tends to be exhibited the great quantity of the linguistic form. In the viewpoint of Cognitive Linguistics, the semantics is no doubt a conceptionalist semantics. That is, meaning resides in conceptualization, broadly interpreted as including any aspect of our mental experience. The generalization by Haiman (1983: 801 – 802) from a cognitive perspective goes that the more complex a concept is, the longer a linguistic expression is or "the more complex an expression, the more complex and deep its intention." Lakoff and Johnson (1980: 127) understand it as a container metaphor, agreeing that given linguistic expressions are containers and their meanings are the content of those containers: the more of form is the more of content. This opinion is also approvingly mentioned in Plank (1979), Anttila (1989), Newmeyer (1998a) and Itkonen (2004). Givón (1990) has formulated the Quantity Principle in a functional way:

(34) a. A larger chunk of information will be given a larger chunk of code.
b. Less predictable information will be given more coding material.
c. More important information will be given more coding material. (pp. 969 - 973)

The first Principle of Quantity can be reflected in multi-event descriptions which tend to be longer than single-event descriptions. Look at the following examples:

(35) a. He slept, then got up.
b. He slept. (Givón 1985: 50)

Comparatively speaking, the chunk of code or linguistic structure of sentence (35a) is relatively longer than that of sentence (35b). Sentence (35a) bears more information as it contains two events, whereas sentence (35b) bearing one event reveals less information. Furthermore, Principle (34b) can be shown in the larger size of lexical words implying less predictable information, as shown in (36):

(36) a. Joe told Bill, then *he told* Sally.
b. Joe told Bill and then [ϕ] Sally. (Givón 1985: 50)

Seen form the sentence (36b), the subject + verb constituent "*he told*" had been removed leaving the direct object "Sally" remained. Functional explanation may go to the idea that the reduced expression is in fact the "old" or "known" information and without any necessity to be repeated. Cognitively speaking, the reduced expression of more predictable information in (36b) is in general an icon of the less attention that is paid to such information. Principle (34c) can be well verified in the passive and anti-passive voices in English:

(37) a. John drank *the beer* in a hurry.

b. *The beer* was drunk in a hurry.

c. John drinks a lot [ϕ]. (Kim 1999: 257)

It is observed that, compared to the sentence given in (37a), sentence (37c) differs from sentence (37a) in the aspect that the direct object referent "the beer" is dropped in sentence (37c). Reasonable explanation can go that the information is unnecessary to be encoded into the textual structure if it does not represent as important in information processing chain. On the contrary, the noun phrase "the beer", originally located in the direct object position in sentence (37a), has been moved to the place of subject referent in sentence (37b) when the information becomes significant and needs to be encoded in the most profiling way within a sentential structure. Consequently, the original sentence has been passivized in the form designated in (37b).

The proposal of Quantity Principle has long been an important aspect of Markedness Theory (Givón 1995) in Discourse Analysis. Marked forms or constituents are typically more complicated or longer than unmarked ones in linguistic structures and semantically more sophisticated as well. The following conversations are good cases in point.

(38) A: Let's get kids something.

B: Okay. But I veto I-C-E-C-R-E-A-M-S.

(39) A: What does your brother do?

B: My brother is a disturber of the piano keys. (Song 2006: 126)

Speaker B in conversation (38) spells out the letters of the nominal phrase "*ice creams*" instead of articulating it directly. The structural complexity may lead the listener to pondering about the motivated reason for producing marked structure in speech and taking his or her time to think of the intention added to the typical answer. It closely accords to the Quantity Principle: when the code chunk becomes larger, the message is less predictable and the hearer has to put more cognitive efforts to construe the inference. In the same way, speaker B in conversation (39) describes the occupation of his brother by choosing a sentimental nominal phrase "*a disturber of the piano keys*" other than by directly saying "*my brother is a pianist.*" The complicated language codes are used to make the information semantically more salient and more highlighting. Thus one of the effective methods to achieving emphasis in language is to make the structure/form marked.

3.2.3. Sequential Order Principle

Works focusing on the analysis of chronological sequences in linguistic structures have been done previously in the interpretation of literariness in terms of schema theory[①] (de Beaugrande and Dressler 1981). In a text chunk, there is temporal or spatial diagrammaticity of connectedness, if coherence is reflected on the level of expression by syntactic or lexical cohesion.

The sequence of clauses can iconically correspond to the order of the occurrence of

① According to de Beaugrande and Dressler (1981:383 – 422), schema theory states that organized knowledge is an elaborate network of abstract mental structure. Main principles of this theory include: 1) teach general knowledge and broad concepts; 2) build on the knowledge and make connections between ideas; 3) prior knowledge is necessary for new knowledge; 4) schemata will change as new information is acquired; 5) schemata are organized in a meaningful way.

the depicted events without the help of those visible cohesive devices. These properties are again present in Caesar's famous Latin phrase: "Vēnī, vīdī, vīcī.", meaning in English "I came, I saw, I conquered." The three clauses are ordered into a coherent discourse because they correspond to the temporal order of the scenes in our experience. Haiman (1985a) explains language in the way that may iconically display the temporal or conceptual asymmetry of coordinate conjoined elements. Givón (1990: 971 – 972) observes the semantic and pragmatic principles of the natural sequential order. In this study, temporal and spatial sequence orders are to be elaborated.

3.2.3.1. Temporal order

Majority of the classical linguistic examples following the temporal order reside in the narratives. Haiman (1985b: 4) mentions that the order of clauses in a narrative correspond to the order of events that they describe. It is widely acknowledged that few languages, if any, at least not yet up to now, are known to have their stories told with the narrative sequence being the reverse of the chronological order. Virtanen (1992: 114, 117) notes that temporal sequentiality, seen as the most widespread phenomenon of iconicty, is the fundamental characteristics of the narrative type of text. Experiential sequence of the reality in the world, as a discourse motivating factor, will determine the linear order of the narrative statement.

Greenberg (1963: 103), who takes a cognitive attitude towards the explanation, claims that "the order of elements in language parallels that in physical experience or the order of knowledge." The iconic exploitation of temporal order is also Saussure's "linearity of the linguistic sign", a property which Saussure considers no less essential than its arbitrariness. Under the same claim, Jakobson (1975) maintains that the relationship of the co-occurring elements of two sentences corresponds to the relationships of the two events that actually happen in the real life. Extending to the other linguistic levels, Newmeyer (1998b: 117) has noted that the order of morphemes or even lexemes tends to reflect logical relationships among their referents, after which the strong tendency to ordering clauses in coherent discourse is described by Givón (1990: 971), "The order of clauses in coherent discourse tends to correspond to the temporal order of the occurrence of the depicted events." Take the following sentences into consideration:

(40) a. He opened the door, came in, sat and ate.

b. * He sat, came in, ate and opened the door. (Givón 1985: 54)

Sentence (a) in example (40) is acceptable because the order of small clauses in the utterance resembles the order of actions involved in actual experience. Those that break the law of temporal succession tend to be regarded as ungrammatical like the given sentence (40b). Consider more examples:

(41) a. He had an accident and remained wounded.

b. * He remained wounded and had an accident.

Sentence (41a) is preferable to sentence (41b) for the reason that it is in accordance with the *cause and effect* order of the naturally occurring sequence of the accident. On the surface, coordinate clauses are such that clause A proceeds the clause B as it is taken as indicating the cause of clause B. In effect, there lies a profound conceptually motivated relation between causal and temporal succession, in the sense that what is first in temporal order can be plausibly assumed as the cause of what is the second.

3.2.3.2. Spatial order

Many researchers have noted a systematic correspondence between the domains of time and space in language. Time is often talked in terms of space, such as "A theory was proposed ahead of its time." As a matter of fact, a spatial order principle needs to be first traced before temporal order to account for word order in linguistic representations because spatial order is the most basic of all to reflect the human cognitive mechanism.

Similar to the temporal order, linguistic structures often iconically represent the spatial order of natural entities in the universe. For instance, because humans perceive themselves as upright beings, vertical directionality is physically and psychologically established by our experience to be the most salient of the spatial dimensions. In addition, humans move over the surface of the earth. The horizontal dimensions have a great impact on the linear ordering concept. Both vertical and horizontal dimensions are mental perceptions from the universe. When they are projected into linguistic structures, spatial orders are viewed as icons of experience in the real world. Compare (a) and (b) sentences in the following two examples which apparently reveal the spatial concepts of human beings.

(42) a. No. 800, University Avenue, Carbondale, Illinois, USA

b. 美国 伊利诺伊州 卡本黛尔市,大学路,800 号

(* USA, Illinois, Carbondale, University Avenue, No. 800)

(43) a. That book is on the 12th shelf in the Western Language Section on the seventh floor in the library.

b. 那本书在图书馆七楼西语部第十二排书架上

(* That book is in the library on the seventh floor, in the Western Language Section on the 12th shelf.)

When writing the address, Americans are inclined to the way of spatial description from the specific to the general location as is shown in example (42a), while the reverse is the Chinese tendency like what has been given in the example (42b): from the general to the specific location. The same happens in English and Chinese existential sentences (43a) and (43b). The different locating approach in different cultures can be accounted for the different perceptual and conceptualizing mechanism of space in different speech communities.

3.3. Summary

Saussure's arbitrariness causes a stir on successive scholars in understanding the relations between linguistic structures and conceptual systems. Nevertheless, these experts did not stop upholding him until the last two decades of the past century, when the idea that language is highly iconic of the world gets the upper hand and Saussure meets his Waterloo. Consequently, an increasing number of linguists tend to accept a complementary relation between arbitrariness and iconicity.

The belief in the present study goes to the theory of iconicity and its convincing studies as well because the achievement of iconicity has well demonstrated that in many cases, language is proved to be highly motivated and that its powerful explanatory force has got involved in nearly a diversity of linguistic structure forms, and even in various scopes of language. In so doing, it is undoubtfully believed that the distinction between arbitrariness and iconicity is not a clear-cut but a matter of degree. Every sign is possibly arbitrary but definitely iconic of the concept or the conceptual structure in real life. The question to be laid attention to is to what degree the linguistic sign is iconized.

We also believe in Haiman's statement (1985a) that iconically motivated signs may lose their motivation gradually as conventionalization comes in, while culture and way of thinking have presupposed the influence of iconicity in different language systems. Haiman (1985a: 11) holds that at any stage of any natural language, the originally iconically motivated patterns have been obscured by various kinds of destructions that economy entails, under the headings of simplification or reduction, distortion. And it is likely that arbitrariness "creeps into" languages to de-iconize or conventionalize their iconically motivated characters. There is a well-documented tendency to restore this correlation by a variety of different processes (Haiman 1985a: 5).

The iconicity hypothesis provides people with a powerful external motivation for language structure, and a fresh perspective from which people will not consider language forms to be an entirely autonomous system, or not consider language forms to be independent of meaning if the explicit indications evoke conceptions which merely provide mental access to the linguistic elements. Thus the study of iconicity as a theoretic approach will lead itself to the further understanding of the essence of language, or the relationship between language and reality, cognition, sign and concept, and that as a cognitive tool of language study and learning, iconicity will facilitate language analysis and make the acquisition and the application of foreign language more insightful and efficient.

CHAPTER FOUR AN ICONIC ANALYSIS OF WORD ORDER WITHIN COORDINATE IDIOMS

Having reviewed the literature on word order within coordinate idioms and prenominal modifiers and presenting the iconicity principles as a theoretical framework, it is all ready to seek for the solution to how these word order variations are accounted for relying on the cognitive explanation. For the reason that the coordinate idioms and prenominal modifiers are sequenced in totally distinctive representations, they will have to be explained separately. The linguistic construction focused on in the present chapter is the word order of English and Chinese coordinate idiom phenomena, such as *up and down*, *come and go*. The iconicity principles that enter this chapter are respectively the sequential order principle, spatial order principle and markedness principle as well. The analysis is basically an informational answer to the following three research questions:

a) Are the orderings of the coordinate idioms seen as arbitrary or non-arbitrary?

b) What are the possible relations to iconicity in the orderings of English and Chinese coordinate idioms?

c) What are the explicit cognitive mechanisms for the sequencing of English and Chinese coordinate idioms working behinds the human conceptual system?

The framework of the chapter is designed as follows: the first section covers the definition of coordinate idioms; section two elaborates the ordering features of English and Chinese coordinate idioms from the viewpoint of spatial sequence principle. In the analysis process, the motivations that cause the fixed or unfixed orders in coordinate idioms are addressed and the possible mechanisms are generalized from the point of cognitive and conventional factors. English and Chinese coordinate idioms are further observed from the viewpoint of temporal sequencing in the third section. Section four zooms in the order of those coordinate idioms in English and Chinese that are characteristic of markedness, which is necessarily concerned with when generalizing the explanatory power of ordering linguistic constituents in language. Ultimately, the summary and implications of the analysis are presented.

4. 1. Definition and general properties

Coordinate idioms, what are called as "idiomatic" usages within a language, are the combination of two or more phrasal conjuncts bearing the same syntactic functions but often fixed in the order conveying a single, inclusive meaning, such as the constituent combination "*here and there*", "*head over heels*". A formal definition of coordinate construction is that all phrasal conjuncts are attributed to the same syntactic category and together form a constituent of this category. Quirk et al. (1985:945), for instance, claim that "[we] regard coordination as a type of linkage whereby the resulting conjoint construction is equivalent, structurally speaking, to each of its members." This structure is illustrated in the example "*pizza and pasta*", where the two nouns, "*pizza*" and "*pasta*" form a superordinate noun phrase.① Pinker and Birdsong (1979:497) state that among these expressions, the salient and defining characteristic is the

① Coordinate construction is different from subordinate or dependency constructions because, in the latter, only one constituent (the head) must match the syntactic status of the overall phrase.

linear order born in their constituent terms which are either irreversible or reversible.

These locutions have been referred to by a variety of names in the previous study of the fixed order of the two phrasal conjuncts. For instance, Malkiel (1959) proposes "irreversible binomials" to a pair of words in a fixed and parallel relation. The impressive term "Siamese twins" is defined by Fowler (2003) as a pair of words joined together mostly by coordinators "*and*" or "*or*". In recent years, these coordinate idioms are investigated in the name of freezes by Cooper and Ross (1975).

In general, three types of coordination are distinguished: conjunction or conjunctive coordination, disjunction or disjunctive coordination and adversative coordination. Instances are seen below:

(44) a. the tiger and the lion (conjuctive coordination)

b. the tiger or the lion (disjunctive coordination)

c. He walked fast, but he did not run. (adversative coordination)

Since the focus of the present study is on intra-phrasal phenomena, only conjunctive and disjunctive coordination will be dealt with, because adversative coordination is rare outside clasual coordination (Haspelmath 2004).

It has to be noted that the ordering of the pairs of words can be reversed in many situations, which are looked upon as non-idiomatic constructions. It is not until the past two decades that the reasons that caused unfixed order of certain conjunct pairs have been investigated systematically and theoretically. While the elements are in fixed and idiomatic constructions, the linguistic ordering structure of the two conjuncts involved has to be implicitly in accordance with the particular conceptual structure of community speakers, and the definite linguistic forms naturally fix the meanings that they denote, as is given in (45b) and (46b). Once the order is reversed, the way of revealing meaning by using the opposite order of the linguistic elements is characterized as beneficial to the individual speaker for particular intention in specific situation. In doing so, the inside of a person's mind has to be looked into for his conceptual processing to dig out why human beings have the alternatives of sequence for the word pairs

(45) a. I saw many cats and dogs/dogs and cats on the street.

b. It is raining cats and dogs/ * dogs and cats.

(46) a. Now and then/ Then and now, beer satisfies.

b. Now and then/ * Then and now, it rains.

For the reasons given above, the interest of this research lays emphasis on the order of fixed coordinate constructions, which will be called as coordinate idioms, as opposed to the name called as non-idiomatic constructions when the ordering of constituents are reversible.

Studies in the literature abroad and home seem to be sensitive to the spatial order involved in coordinate idioms and explicitly classify their spatial ordering of the linguistic constituents into three dimensions: vertical, horizontal, and egocentric direction, while merely relating the temporal order to the general correspondence of the natural linear sequence of the entities, actions and events concerned with the people performing in the physical world. In effect, after deeply examining into a body of coordinate idioms, it is found that their order does not necessarily correspond to the natural sequence of activities performed by human beings. In most of the time, human perceptual propensity plays an important role in the working of sequential construction of language constituents. Nevertheless, it is proposed in this study that classifications of temporal ordering in coordinate idioms can be specified into the experiential linear order and the cause-effect/condition-result order, as specific as the classifications of the spatial order. It is further claimed that markedness ordering, as a human perceptual propensity, which used to be considered as a patent in information structure, is in fact a type of iconicity based on human cognitive processing abilities. To put it another way, the present study holds for the idea that the ordering of coordinate idioms is mainly delimited to the temporal sequence, spatial sequence, as well as the markedness sequence worked out through human perceptive and cognitive processing in the course of their interactions with the entities existed in the physical world.

It is also believed that a contrastive study into the sequence of coordinate idioms in two languages can be conducted on account of two reasons. First, many languages have pairs of words arranged in fixed order and parallel relation. Second, certain similarities are potentially shared between two languages, which can be in a large part accounted for in terms of human cognitive systems. Naturally, possible implications are definitely of equal significance if the current study can be extended to the order of coordinate idioms across other languages, such as Korean, French and so on.

4.2. The analysis of coordinate idioms from Temporal Order Principle

In terms of temporal order, only if the linguistic order corresponds to the naturally occurring sequence of human physical activities, it is said to be iconic. The present section provides the substantive evidence to the explanatory value of the temporal order principle by means of both English and Chinese coordinate idiom data①. It expects to uncover other potential motivations on account of their orderings. In addition to the nat-

① The data presented in the study are collected from sources varying from linguistic articles (Malkiel 1959, Cooper and Ross 1975, Allan 1987, Wang 1999, among others) on the prestigious international or national journals to some reference books (Wang 2002, Landsberg 1995). The data sources also include the Oxford English Dictionary and Thesaurus, conversations with native speakers or from the corpus like BNC and COCA. Despite the efforts, it is by no means exhaustive. Inevitably, some odd cases will be encountered and excluded by the researcher after the careful discussion with native speakers.

ural linear order, experiential linear order and cause-effect/condition-result order are added into the temporal order principle. Considerable data manifest that these two types of order principles can also be construed temporally.

4.2.1. Natural linear order in coordinate idioms

As mentioned by Haiman (1985b) in his generalization of the three principles of iconicity, language is structurally adapted to the iconic display of the temporal order. In regard to coordinate idioms, it is greatly acknowledged that the linearity of some coordinate idioms conforms to the linearity of time order in which the event occurs. The temporal linearity is first of all reflected in human descriptions of naturally occurring phenomena, as illustrated in the constituent arrangements① below:

(47) sunrise and sunset; from dawn to dusk; rise and fall; east and west; from beginning to end; first and last; life and death; wax and wane; ancient and present; day and night/ebb and flow

It is customary that people start their working when the sun rises and finish their work and take home to rest when the sun sets. Thus the sequential working arrangement attributes to a factor employed to the description of the phenomenon ordering happening in the nature, like the sunrise before the sunset, the dawn before the dusk, the day before the night and the rise before the fall. Going further, the cognitive generalization of the concept that the sun rises from the east and falls at the west can explain why the element "east" precedes the element "west" in the coordinate idiom "*east and west*".

The words "*beginning*" and "*first*" identically precede the words "*end*" and

① In this section, all examples listed in front of the symbol "/" are the coordinate idioms that correspond to the sequential order principle and those that come after the symbol "/" are the examples violating the sequential order principle but possibly following other conceptual determinants.

"*last*" because all the words "*beginning*", "*first*" and "*end*", "*last*" denote a natural sequence of how things or actions are performed step by step in one's physical experience. Similarly, the noun "*life*" precedes the noun "*death*" because the two words reflect a natural circulation of a person's life and everybody knows it well that after a person is given to birth, he will go through the living process to the destination "*death*". And other coordinate idioms such as "*wax and wane*", "*wear and tear*", "*ancient and present*", all exactly correspond to the natural flow in time from the past to the present until the future. The evidence gained from the data that majority of coordinate idioms conform to the natural linear order is also compatible with corresponding Chinese coordinate idioms. It can be seen in the examples below.

(48) 日出日落（sunrise and sunset）；从早到晚（from dawn to dusk）；有始有终（from beginning to the end）；从生到死（life and death）；月圆月缺（wax and wane）；从古至今（ancient and present）；日日夜夜(day and night)

(49) 潮起潮落（ebb and flow / * flow and cbb ）

It is seen from the examples in (48) that the corresponding Chinese coordinate idioms equally correspond to the linearity of the natural phenomena, leaving the only exception to be the English expression in example (49) "*ebb and flow*". Recall that in Chapter One, stress is laid on the dilemma in which a significant number of linguistic variants frequently cause researchers to suspect the feasibility of an approach or a theory. A possible solution proposed is that there is an assumption of competing motivations. Given several potential motivations, if one is dominant enough over the other, the language will show a variant in the linguistic phenomenon. Given that the syntactic order corresponds to the linear order of the natural events in the actual situation, the word "flow" should precede the word "ebb". The Chinese coordinate idiom does reflect the natural linear order of the act of "*flow*" preceding that of "*ebb*", but the English equivalent is the opposite.

A convincing account from native speakers lies in the phonological preference: disyllable giving way to monosyllable in English, which can be included in the markedness order in the coming section: monosyllable is less marked than disyllable (Allan 1987: 72). Language displays the word order variant due to the fact that the natural linear iconic order has lost its competition against the phonological rules. Of course, the phonological rules cannot be presented and supported by no less than one single example. In effect, many coordinate idioms reflect this rule, as given in (50).

(50) gas and electric; bread and butter; nuts and raisins; bows and arrows;
lions and tigers; prim and proper; horse and rider; shoes and stockings;
goose and gander

The phonological rule is preferred because of its sequential order principle: "*less complex to complex*". If the conjuncts of an idiom consist of two monosyllables, the ordering principle "the short monosyllable going before the longer monosyllable" can borrow the identical reason, as illustrated below:

(51) safe and sound; sun and surf; sea and ski; fair and square; bill and coo;
cat and mouse; fits and starts; duck and drake; trick or treat

The English coordinate idiom "*trick or treat*" is particularly interesting because it is regarded as disjunctive idiom existing in the general form "A or B" with the coordinator "or" rather than "and" denoting the meaning of being alternative, as in (52):

(52) a. A or B = If not A, then B.

If it is the case, the English idiom "*trick or treat*" should be reversed into "treat or trick", meaning "If you do not give us a treat, we will play a trick on you." However, according to Cooper and Ross (1975), instead of following the condition-result linear order, the order of the two conjuncts is appropriate by following the phonological law: the short vowel [i] precedes the long vowel [i:]. Despite of the exceptional examples, an abundance of data can be listed to verify the linear order of natural phenomena in both English and Chinese coordinate idioms.

4.2.2. Experiential linear order

Greenberg (1963: 103) claimed that it is often the case that "the order of elements in language parallels that in physical experience or the other of knowledge." Enkvist (1981) held the same view and observed,

> "Certain aspects of linear ordering in texts must be viewed as icons of experience① [...] Correspondingly, when decoding texts we actually tend to maximize their information by interpreting linear order as an exponent of temporal, spatial, causal or socially conditioned order... (p. 97)"

Enkvist (1981) posits his perspectives beyond the sentential explanation to the analysis of text and discourse. Indeed, in many instances within sentences, language is manipulated to be isomorphic with the order of human experiences. In the point of human social activities, a person's behaviors are usually continuous and enduring chains of actions. The over-all linguistic structures are supposed to have the same arrangements as human non-verbal behaviors in the universe. Coordinate idioms, being a part of linguistic structures, reflect the pictorial structures of human experiential activities in the real world, as exemplified below.

---

① Enkvist (1981:97 – 111) initiates the notion "Experiential Iconicism", referring to the ways in which "elements of language are ordered to make a text isomorphic with the universe it describes."

(53) bow and scrape; cut and thrust; cut and run; hit and run; hit and miss; cut and carve; divide and rule; out and about; wait and see; scissors and paste; knife and fork; forgive and forget; near and dear; wear and tear; push and shove; comb and brush

When people behave to follow experiential sequences in real life, the expressions used to display the action chains like those idioms in (53) are all iconic of the universal sequence they describe. Any reversed form can make no sense to hearers or audience. As the examples show, people must perform the action of bowing before they scrape. In front of their enemy, the act of "cut" must come off before the verb "thrust" denoting the act of pushing suddenly or violently in a specified direction. People will disapprove the ordering of being able to relax "about" before one's going "out" of his or her house. The word orderings in the idioms like "*wait and see*", "*scissors and paste*", and "*knife and fork*" are more acceptable and expressive, because of the fact that "people cannot always sharply predict the result on the cause-effect chain of an event if they do not wait patiently to see it"; "people can only paste after they use the scissors to cut the paper into pieces"; "it is thought as a good manner for a customer to use a knife to cut the beef before he or she uses a fork to eat it at a table." Furthermore, if we are wronged by people, it keeps lingering on our mind until we finally forget it. As for the idiom "*near and dear*", it is also seen as mimetic of the human experience in the world because one has to stay close to each other before they become beloved ones. In so doing, the rest of the examples are easy to be conceptually processed by any person who lives and possesses the social or experiential fundamentals. The corresponding Chinese expressions given below help to better understand the order of these coordinate idioms of which people are miming the sequences of the events that happen in the experiential world.

(54) 鞠躬作揖 (bow and scrape); 短兵相接 (cut and thrust); 断矛逃跑 (cut and run);

肇事逃逸（hit and run）；切割（cut and carve）；参与策划（divide and rule）；
外出转转（out and about）；等着瞧（wait and see）；剪贴（scissors and paste）；
刀与叉（knife and fork）；原谅忘记（forgive and forget）；亲近密切（near and dear）；
推搡（push and shove）；梳刷（comb and brush）

Looking into the expressions selected, it becomes immediately transparent that all Chinese equivalents share the same sequence with the English coordinate idioms. In a nutshell, the orders of both Chinese and English coordinate idioms all represent the processing sequence people experience in the physical world. This indicates the universal principle employed by the people in both countries when they use language to reflect the sequences of human experiential perception in the entity world.

4.2.3. Cause-effect /Condition-result order

Jakobson (1975) noted that any human behavior is goal-directed. The close correspondence between linguistic phenomena and human behavioral structures requires that language coding denotes the characters of cause, purpose or condition and result in human activities. With the preferred order, the form of the expression is miming the semantic relations of the events. Thus, the temporal sequence can be found in the sequential order of cause-effect, condition-result or purpose-goal chains in the factual social activities. Some supportive English examples are considered as follows:

(55) cause and effect; trial and error; tried and true; slow and steady; high and dry; give and take; pain and gain; pick and mix; cash and carry; forgive and forget; crime and punishment; hope and pray; bigger and better

Listed here are the English coordinate idioms that are iconic of the linear order of *cause before effect chain* or *condition before result chain* designated in an event. For instance, we will finally know whether or not we make mistakes merely after we try it.

Thus we have the idiom "*trial and error*". People tend to use the coordinate "*give and take*" because it is a moral belief that a person has the privilege to take under the condition that he is given out and benefits others. It is always a rule that we can never amount to anything before we take painstaking efforts into it; only if things have been picked up, we can perform the act of mixing them up. It is also socially conventionalized that you cannot take the commodities away from shop if you don't pay in cash or credit card. Suppose a person commits a crime, he is definitely punished by the law. And in western countries, Christian parents will always let their children know that if they hope or desire for a thing, they will pray to God for getting it as a Christmas gift.

After a considerable number English instances have been proved, it is natural that the next question to be asked is whether Chinese expressions carry the same cause-effect, condition-result or purpose-goal order. Consider the examples below:

(56)因果（cause and effect），实践证实（tried and true），慢而稳（slow and steady）；
曲高和寡（high and dry）；给予索取（give and take）；付出收获（pain and gain）；
现金取货（cash and carry）；罪与罚（crime and punishment）；越大越好（bigger and better）；
不念旧恶(forgive and forget)

It goes without saying that Chinese coordinate idioms, similar to English expressions, have the same arrangements of *cause effect/condition result* order of human natural logic. Notice in the last Chinese version "不念旧恶", the direct object has been added after the two verbs "*forgive*" and "*forget*" in that Confucius idea that has been penetrated in Chinese culture suggests that those evil deeds done by evil persons should be forgiven and forgotten by people, while helps or supports from others can never be forgotten.

In the analysis of the sequential order of both English and Chinese coordinate idioms, it can be generalized that the arrangement frame in the expressions of the two countries do accord to the linear order of natural phenomena in universe, temporal order of human behaviors in the experiential world, and the cause-effect/condition-result order of human activities. It reveals that both English and Chinese share the same cognitive processing when composing sequence-based expressions. This explanation truly provides convincing proof to the syntactic iconicity of coordinate idioms.

4.3. The analysis of coordinate idioms from Spatial Order

Although all the linguistic features in the aforesaid section can be explained by virtue of the natural order in the universe or physical world, there may be some grain of features that do not appear identical with our experiential world, or that have no answer. It is oriented from the "inner relationship" between the sign and its signified object, which has become infinitely complex from Plato on.

Syntactic iconicity regarding to linguistic structures posits far more than the simple classic referential view that word orders are necessarily corresponding to physical structure of the things in its extra-linguistic world, but a view holding that:

"A very simple structure of that relationship which can be called 'meaning': [where] linguistic and extra-linguistic facts are naturally and necessarily linked without any intervening psychological mechanism (Hörmann 1971: 149)."

Indeed, it is the claim of the principles underlying coordinate idioms that psychological mechanism does intervene and motivate linguistic structures. The correlation to spatial order in language cannot be identified without human psychological mechanism.

4.3.1. Egocentric order

In considering the spatial order, the coordinate idioms that are easy to come to our minds are "*here and there*", "*this and that*", and "*come and go*". There comes the question: why should the spatial dexis "*here*" be placed before "*there*"; the determiner "*this*" come off before "*that*"; and the motion verb "*come*" have to go first and "*go*" later? In the service of the explanation to this kind of idioms, Lyons (1979) proposed the term *the canonical situation of utterance*, which means,

> "egocentric in the sense that the speaker, by virtue of being the speaker, casts himself in the role of ego and relates everything to his viewpoint. He is at the zero-point of the spatiotemporal coordinates of what we will refer to as the deictic context ... Egocentricity is temporal as well as spatial, since the role of speaker is being transferred from one participant to the other as the conversation proceeds, and the participants may move around as they are conversing: the spatiotemporal zero-point (the *here* and *now*) is determined by the place of the speaker at the moment of utterance... (p. 638)"

Humanity is described to establish concepts in the universe, where the person is his/her own frozen dimension. Indeed, people perennially perceive of themselves from the vantage point of the canonical situation of utterance, a so-called face-to-face situation for sender and receiver, wherein, moreover, the sender perceives of himself/herself as always the center of the universe. For example, the English determiners like "*this*" and "*these*" are designed to refer to things relatively close to the speaker in distance, while the equivalents "*that*" and "*those*" referring to those afar from the speaker in distance. Owing to preference to the human egocentricity in perception, the ordering in certain coordinate idioms is irreversible. Egocentricity, described by Lyons (1979), is spatial as well as temporal, because we always start from where we are, conceiving ourselves as the zero-point, both in space and time. Therefore, such serials as shown in (57) exist in language.

(57) this and that; here and there; these and those; now and then; come and go;

inside and outside; today and tomorrow; at home and abroad; domestic and abroad; sooner or later; back and forth; to and fro①; inhale and exhale; hither and thither; in and out; tomorrow and the day after

All these idioms are characteristic of being egocentric in nature, because their cognitive constraints displayed on these expressions can be understood like this: the speaker, taking the advantage of being the producer of the utterance, casts himself/herself in the center of the universe and relates everything to his/her viewpoint. He is at the zero-point of the spatio-temporal expressions.

Recall that Cooper and Ross (1975: 63 – 111) have proposed the so-called "Me-first" principle, among which the pronoun "*me*" is taken as the reference point in space and the moment the person is speaking as the reference point in time. This yields the above-mentioned, rigorously ordered conjuncts. In this sense, it is believed in this study that "Me-first" principle is identical with egocentric order principle and can be described as a powerful explanation of egocentric order. The same order can be found in the corresponding Chinese idioms.

(58)这个那个 (this and that); 这里那里 (here and there); 这些那些 (these and those); 此时彼时 (now and then); 来来去去 (come and go); 里里外外 (inside and outside);

今天明天 (today and tomorrow); 国内国外 (at home and abroad);

这儿那儿 (hither and thither); 进进出出 (in and out); 明后天 (tomorrow and the day after)

① The English coordinate idioms "back and forth" and "to and fro" refer to their special usages with motion verbs "come" and "go" in compounds, such as "come back and go forth" and "come to and go fro", which indicates moving towards or from the speaker. In this sense, they are well explained by the egocentric order of syntactic iconicity.

The ordering compatibility of the elements within English and Chinese coordinate idioms adds proof to the announcement that the arrangement of coordinate idioms in both languages, and maybe among more languages, is orderly and deeply rooted in the egocentric or me-first principle.

4.3.2. Vertical order

Humans perceive of themselves as upright beings moving over the surface of the earth. Accordingly, many scholars point out that vertical way of ordering verbal presentation can be the most basic altitude of observing directional natural phenomena in the real world. As Landsberg (1987: 240) once stated that the perceptual principle of "*head up first/feet down second*" is a strong determinant factor on our linguistic sequential order. Moreover, Lyons (1979) similarly claimed that the vertical orientation is firmly grounded in our understanding of the Law of Gravity and the fact like the "*heaven is up/the earth is down*". His opinion is clearly shown in the statement given below:

> "This gives us the means of identifying one of the dimensions in a three-dimensional space; it also gives us a fixed zero-point at the ground-level. Furthermore, directionality in the vertical dimension-i. e. the difference between upwards and downwards [...] is established by our experience of the effects of the force of gravity, by the fact that, normally, the sky is above us and the ground beneath us and by the asymmetry of the human body in the vertical dimension. For these, and the other reasons, verticality is physically and psychologically the most salient of the spatial dimensions: linguistically as we shall see, it is the primary dimension [...] (p. 690)"

If it is indeed the most salient spatial dimension physically and psychologically, it is inevitably the most fundamental principle of sequencing linguistic structures like "*head up first/feet down second*", without an exclusion of the ordering of coordinate idioms. In English data searched in a variety of sources, an abundant number of examples can be found and listed.

(59) above and below; on and under; up and down; high and low; top and bottom; from top to toe; from head to toe; heaven and earth; heaven and hell; mountains and seas; hands and feet; heads and tails; arms and legs; fingers and toes; tooth and nail; bra and pants; hat and coat; hands and knees

To testify the habitual tendency in the way of using the above mentioned idioms rather than a linguistic conventionalization of a speech community, a great number of psychological experimentations have been conducted in the 1970s, among which the empirical research conducted by Clark (1973) is by far the most influential. He discovered that in the minds of subjects, the direction denoted by the word "*above*" is conceptually more salient than that denoted by the word "*below*". Along the same line, the prepositions, adverbs, and even adjectives like "*on*", "*up*" and "*high*" all perceptually come before the words indicating the direction of being "*downwards*", naming "*under*", "*down*" and "*low*". The results from the experimentation surprisingly are in accordance with the vertical order opinion sponsored by linguists. In Chinese, the same directional expressions are given in (60).

(60) 上上下下 (above and below; on and under; up and down); 上面下面 (top and bottom);
高高低低 (high and low); 从上到下 (from top to toe); 从头到脚 (from head to toe);
首尾 (heads and tails); 天与地 (heaven and earth); 天堂地狱 (heaven and hell);
山川河流 (mountains and seas); 手足 (hands and feet); 胳膊腿 (arms and legs);
手指脚趾 (fingers and toes); 内衣短裤 (bra and pants); 手脚膝盖 (hands and knees)

It is evident that all the Chinese examples exhibit the common sequence with corresponding English version due to the universal psychological or perceptual propensity of the principle "*head up first/feet down second*".

4. 3. 3. Horizontal Order

We perceive the world of a three-dimension but not of a one-dimension unity. Consequently, in addition to perceiving the entities in the vertical order, the horizontal dimension has an equally great impact on the ordering of coordinate idioms in both languages. Lyons (1979) again points out,

> "Man is asymmetrical in one of the two horizontal dimensions, and symmetrical in the other: i. e. he has a front and a back, and two symmetrical sides. He has his principal organs of perception directed towards the region in front of him: he normally moves in the direction in which he is facing, and when he interacts with his fellows, he does so, in what has been felicitously described as the canonical encounter (Clark 1973), by confronting them. " (p. 691)

It is concluded that Lyons sorts out two types of horizontal dimensions: the asymmetrical one (i. e. *front and back*) and, the symmetrical① one (i. e. *right and left*). The asymmetricality② of our perceptual horizontal dimensions as is implied that the things placing in the *front* direction are conceptually regarded as more significant, more salient, and hence people opt to think and speak *front first*, as exemplified below.

---

① Unlike Lyons, Schachter (1977) argues for the existence of *a coordinate construction constraint*, which said that "the two constituents of a coordinate construction must be the same syntactic category and have the same semantic function. The conveyed meaning remains unchanged even though the orders of the conjuncts are reversed. In this way they are semantically and formally symmetrically. "(Haiman 1985b: 86) Apparently, Schachter didn't take a cognitive account into the semantic understanding of the coordinate idioms.

② Asymmetricality in Syntax implies that the order of the two clauses corresponds to the order of the depicted events and any reversing of the two clauses' order can lead to the semantic difference. Thus the different temporal sequence of the clauses is an iconically asymmetrical use of language.

(61) front and behind; before and after; front and back; fore and after; front to back; bow and stern; front and rear

The idiom "*front* or *before*" indicates the direction that people normally orient towards, and the temporal preference when people conduct their communication with one another. Therefore, it is regarded as the readily-reached spatial and temporal orientation. Similar to English expressions, the "*front*" direction in those Chinese idioms is also seen as more salient and more preferable than the "*back*" direction. The following examples can back up the viewpoint.

(62) 前前后后 (front and back; front and behind); 先后 (before and after); 之前之后 (fore and after); 从前到后 (front to back); 船头船尾 (bow and stern); 首尾 (front and rear)

Under certain circumstances, our perceptual saliency of directionality is somewhat weaker than when we concern the horizontal direction of "*front before behind*". A good case in point is the idiom used by people "*right and left*". Perhaps it is for this reason that the English linguistic structures tend to go from "*right*" *to* "*left*", while in Chinese expression, perceptual and conceptual habit favors the movement from "*left*" to "*right*". Lyons (1979) has further observed,

> "The asymmetrical front-back dimension is less salient than the vertical dimension, but more salient than the symmetrical right-left dimension. Linguistically, the front-back dimension, then, is the second dimension." (p. 691)

Given the three dimensions of human perceptual and psychological world, the degree of asymmetrical saliency is much valued: the vertical dimension is strong in the asymmetrical saliency; the front-back dimension relatively less strong; the right-left dimension is rather weak in linguistic saliency. In other words, for composing linguistic structures, the vertical dimension is the easiest to be arranged for due to its salient asymmetrical direction, while the right-left dimension is the least accessible for its weak degree of saliency. Consider the following English idioms.

(63) a. height and width; latitude and longitude; top right corner; bottom left corner; high and wide; short and fat;

b. * width and height; * longitude and latitude; * right top corner; * left bottom corner; * wide and high; * fat and short

In English and other Indo-European languages, the points of the compass are given in the order "*North- South- East- West*", whereas in Chinese, they are given in the order "*East-West-South-North*". The interesting thing is that the sequence "*East first, West second*" is different from the sequence of "*North*" and "*South*" in some respects: "E*ast West*" follows the sequence of sunrise and sunset, dawn and dusk, etc (Allan 1987: 56), which are easily identified by human beings living on the earth. In contrast, the distinction between "*North*" and "*South*", similar to "*right and left*" which is a symmetrical direction from a two-dimension perceptual perspective is by no means a salient directional pair easy for people to identity. Thus different cognitive preferences are shown in different countries.

4.4. An analysis of coordinate idioms from Markedness Order

Birdsong (1995: 31) argues that the linearity in human languages is attributed to three determinant factors: markedness considerations, information-processing constraints and iconic mechanisms. He presents that various types of evidence converge on the conclusion that the factors of iconicity, markedness and cognitive processing constraints conspire to determine aspects of linear order in linguistic structures.

Though his idea that three determinants affect the linear form in languages is agreeable, Birdsong's markedness considerations can in effect be incorporated into the sequential order principle of iconicity. As far as coordinate idioms are concerned, the former two sections have demonstrated how iconicity and cognitive processing can determine their sequential order. The task of this section is to collect enough data to verify that the order of markedness issue can exert influence on coordinate idioms as equal as what iconicity does. Actually, I intend to demonstrate that the markedness principle is identically iconic of the human cognitive, conceptual, experiential world, and it is considered an idiosyncratic iconicity of human cognitive processing.

The markedness order is formerly used to explain information structure in discourse. The order from unmarked element to marked element in an English expression usually corresponds to how the information goes naturally within a text. The fact that *unmarked* precedes *marked* is mainly because the unmarked is more common than the marked and much easier to be employed in language phenomena, while the marked form implies extraordinary, additional, salient or less accessible meaning in information processing. To be put in the cognitive framework, the unmarked information always needs less cognitive attention or processing time, while marked information requires relatively more intense attention or longer time before it is interpreted. In this sense, iconicity becomes a basic constituent to evaluate or measure unmarked or marked in information structure.

Indeed, the iconic consideration into markedness is by far a new one. Givón (1990) has ever proposed two rules to distinguish the marked from the unmarked in a cognitive scope:

(64) i. Structural complexity.

The marked structure tends to be more complex or larger than the corresponding unmarked one.

ii. Cognitive complexity.

The marked category tends to be cognitively more complex in terms of attention, mental effort and/or the processing time than the unmarked one. (p. 947)

The significance of the rules is that the marked structure is most of time complex in syntactic forms, and the syntactic complexity of the marked structures correspondingly reflects the semantic or cognitive complexity in conceptual structures. Marked forms or structures bear structurally and semantically more complex meanings and more complicated cognitive processing in conceptualizing the meanings than unmarked forms. In this respect Givón gives the remarks that markedness is the so-called principle of "the most general facet of iconicity in syntax" (p. 947), equal to its role in markedness theory. As a result, they are cognitively more difficult to be interpreted than unmarked forms. Support is lent to the current point by the following illustrations. Reduplicative plurals illustrate iconicity of complexity in an obvious way, and any modification or elaboration of one meaning-bearing grammatical element by another leads to the increase of both types of complexity. In the realm of syntax, conceptual and structural complexity tends to go hand in hand (Newmeyer 1998b: 117). It is evident that the unmarked-marked order corresponds to the order principle of iconicity.

4.4.1. The unmarked-marked order

The notion of unmarked-marked principle enters structural linguistics via the Prague School (Givón 1990: 945). The Pragueans state that in a pair of entities, one member is definitely possessing the presence of one or more properties, whereas the other possessing its absence. Under this framework, the former one is usually defined as the unmarked element that has comparatively general meanings and usages; the latter, the marked element which is the one that has unconventional meanings or distinctive features.

The explanation that the nature of markedness leaves its mark on grammatical structures comes from the fact that language is used to communicate and communication involves the conveying of information that appropriately contains semantic complexity or additional content. In addition, the assignment of markedness also suggests that linguistic markedness is the product of interaction between the perceptual and the cultural aspect of cognition, like Edmondson (1985) states:

> "Freezes should be considered 'conventionally ordered pairs' or 'rigorously ordered series of lexical terms,' in which the first element 'tends to be the unmarked or prototypical element ...' in English we say *day and night* and not *night and day*, unless we wish to underline in a marked way the continued striving or persisting of something. (p. 124)"

In accounting for this respect, Mayerthaler (1981) and Dressler et al (1987: 67) invoke the principle of "*perceptual accessibility*", which can be employed to explain the ordering of the English coordinate idioms,

> "The first of these elements represents the prototype of category, whereas the second represents the less prototypical, i. e. is more marked [...] In short, one can establish ordered pairs of values of semantic or cognitive categories [...] The perceptually more accessible, i. e. earlier perceived, pole in a category is on the left. (p. 13)"

Landsberg (1995: 71) has generalized several criteria defined as the familiarity or saliency hierarchy of human cognition from a semantic point of view. Here they are considered to be iconic of the unmarked-marked order principle and more criteria are added to the marked order (i. e. (65e), (65f) and (65g)).

(65) a. animate precedes inanimate

b. human precedes animate

c. adult precedes adolescence

d. male precedes female

e. chief precedes accessorial

f. visible precedes invisible

g. singular precedes plural

All the criteria here can be viewed as sub-criteria of a general criterion which fulfill the iconic function, namely, a criterion in which cognitively unmarked element precedes the marked. The tendency for *animate* references to precede *inanimate*, *human* references to precede *animate*, *adult* references to precede *adolescent*, etc. is dominant in English coordinate idioms, as respectively shown in (66a) - (66g) below.

(66) a. man and machine; man and nature; life and death; live or die;
body and soul; flora and fauna; heart and soul; people and things;
animal or vegetable

b. beauty and beast; man and beast; man and dog; man and god

c. father and son; mother and daughter; teacher and student; old and young;
like father, like son; master and apprentice; son and grandson; man and boy;
parent and child; cow and calf; cat and kitten; mare and foal /father and grandfather

d. Mr. and Mrs. ; he and she; father and mother; boys and girls; man and woman;
man and boy; king and queen; husband and wife; Adam and Eve; papa and mama;
grandfather and grandmother; brothers and sisters; boyfriend and girlfriend/
aunts and uncles; bride and groom; goose and gander; duck and drake;
moms and dads; ladies and gentlemen

e. watch and chain; bow and arrow; lock and key; a needle and thread;
cup and saucer; milk and water; milk and honey; bread and butter;
cups and gold; bed and board; gin and tonic, rum and coke;
highways and byways; coffee and cake; dine and wine

f. heart and soul; flesh and soul; day and night; bright and dark

g. one and all; ham and eggs; cheese and crackers; one or two; whole and parts; head and shoulders; head and ears; hand and fingers; skull and crossbones; meat and potatoes; fox and hounds; hammer and tongs; bra and pants; Mick Jagger and the Rolling Stones; monolingual and bilingual; unidirectional and bidirectional; once or twice; beer and skittles; dust and ashes; foot and toes

Semantically speaking, the noun "*man*" has the semantic features [+ human] and [+ male]. These features can make the word "*man*" prototypical either in the animate category or in the human category. Thus "*man*" precedes "*animal*", "*woman*" and "*thing*" as well. Based on this explanation, the ordering of the idiom "*man and dog*" is plausibly following an unmarked-marked order, whereas " * *dog and man*" is not. The corresponding Chinese expressions also conform to the unmarked-marked order. They are provided as follows.

(67) a. 人与机器 (man and machine); 人与自然 (man and nature); 生命地球 (life and earth);

生与死 (life and death); 身心 (body and soul); 动植物 (flora and fauna);

心灵 (heart and soul); 人与事物 (people and things); 动物与植物 (animal or vegetable)

b. 美女野兽 (beauty and beast); 人与兽 (man and beast); 人与狗 (man and dog); 人与上帝 (man and god)

c. 父亲儿子 (father and son); 母亲儿子 (mother and daughter); 老师学生 (teacher and student); 老少长幼 (old and young); 有其父必有其子 (like father, like son), 师徒 (master and apprentice)

d. 先生女士 (Mr. and Mrs.); 父亲母亲 (father and mother); 男孩女孩 (boys and girls); 男人女人 (man and women); 国王王后 (king and queen); 丈夫妻子 (husband and wife); 亚当夏娃 (Adam and Eve); 爸妈 (papa and mama); 爷爷奶奶 (grandfather and grandmother); 兄弟姐妹 (brothers and sisters); 男朋友女朋友 (boyfriends and girlfriends)/ 爸爸妈

妈（ * dads and moms）；叔叔婶婶（ * uncles and aunts）；先生们女士们（ * gentlemen and ladies）；新郎新娘（ * grooms and bride）；公鹅母鹅（ * goose and gander）；公鸭母鸭（ * duck and drake）

e. 手表手链（watch and chain）；弓箭（bow and arrow）；锁和钥匙（lock and key）；针线（a needle and thread）；杯和托（cup and saucer）；奶水（milk and water）；面包黄油（bread and butter）；掺奎宁水的杜松酒（gin and tonic）；酒水（rum and coke）；饮料茶点（coffee and cake）；吃喝（dine and wine）/ 膳宿（ * board and bed）

f. 心与灵（heart and soul）；肉与灵（flesh and soul）；日夜（day and night）；明暗（bright and dark）

g. 单个整体（one and all）；火腿鸡蛋（ham and eggs）；奶酪饼干（cheese and crackers）；一两个（one or two）；整体部分（whole and parts）；手和肩（head and shoulders）；手和耳（head and ears）；手与手指（hand and fingers）；骷髅骨（skull and crossbones）；牛肉土豆（meat and potatoes）；狐豺（fox and hounds）；锤子钉子（hammer and tongs）；内衣裤（bra and pants）；单双语（monolingual and bilingual）；单双向（unidirectional and bidirectional）；一两次（once or twice）；吃喝（beer and skittles）；尘土（dust and ashes）；脚和脚趾（foot and toes）

We may also notice the controversial sequence between such English items as "*moms and dads*", "*bride and groom*", "*aunts and uncles*", "*ladies and gentlemen*" and the controversial order of their corresponding Chinese versions. English idioms seem interestingly to be the exceptions out of the unmarked-marked principle, for that the noun "*man*" in these coordinate constructions does not take precedent position over the noun "woman" as is mentioned by idealized cognitive model for the social status. Allan (1987) argues that according to the phonological rule of (a pair of) word(s) sequence arrangement: monosyllable before disyllable, the order of the coordinate construction "*bride and groom*" is capable of being understood because the word "*groom*" is the abbreviated form of "*bridegroom*" which is popularly used in Old English in the form of "*bryguma*" *meaning* "*bride's man*" and both of them are unshakably disyllable words. The violation of the "*adult before adolescence*" order in the coordinate constructions like "*father and grandfather*" can identically be identified based on the phonological rule: *monosyllable precedes disyllable.*

As far as the sequence of the other coordinate constructions is concerned, the explanation from Cooper and Ross (1975: 105) is attributed to the principle of "politeness convention". In certain western industrialized countries, people are conditioned to a conceptual propensity that females need to be respected and treated in a polite manner in social circumstances. The cognitive saliency of politeness is purposefully expressed by men of courtesy in these idioms. Thus females are ordered initially not because of perceptual saliency, but rather of conventional saliency.

Chinese coordinate constructions are good cases to oppose it. Different from the cultures of civilized nations, China did not entertain such customs as "Lady first", thus the Chinese counterparts of the above mentioned examples still keep the original male-female order: 爸爸妈妈 (* dads and moms), 叔叔婶婶 (* aunts and uncles), 先生们女士们 (* ladies and gentlemen), etc.

Anomalous to the order of English coordinate idiom "*bed and board*", the reversed order is true for Chinese correspondence. This has been explained to be the fact that considering the ancient Chinese living conditions, food of any kind is thought to be the thing most necessary and essential in the physical world for the reason that in ancient Chinese thoughts, food makes people survive on earth. If no enough food is supplied with, one would encounter hardship, no matter how decent his or her life is and how gracefully s/he has decorated her/his house. In this way, the orders of those Chinese coordinate idioms are considered as having gone through the influence of the Chinese ancient historical philosophical thoughts.

The markedness feature in many languages reflects the natural order of understanding about the relation between a linguistic sign and what it depicted (Hu 1997:4). Psychological experiments with English speakers demonstrate that the natural order of understanding refers to the cognitive process that human beings have undergone when they conceptualize entities in the real living world and the sequence of linguistic representations of a language when they preliminarily acquired as first or second language. That is to say, the concepts that are perceptually animate and cognitively more accessible, are likely to be processed favorably in speakers' mental representations and are definitely mentioned first (Clark and Chase 1974). The linguistic elements represented by these concepts therefore occupy the first place in linguistic arrangement.

The principle of "*unmarked before marked*" suggests that such an ordering should be iconic of the cognitive presentation in that the unmarked items are always more prominent and easier to be understood and acquired and thus they are always first mentioned before the marked ones when people acquire a language. In addition, people also understand the order of some items relying on their psychological tolerance and emotional preference. A good case in point can be referred to those in which the positive item is emotionally chosen first before the negative one.

4.4.2. The positive-negative order

The idea that the positive and negative items in language generally correspond to the unmarked and marked logic has been proved by the psychological experiment (Clark and Clark 1974). The results in the experiment show that children tend to pay more attention to long and reachable objects rather than short and unreachable one; children tend to take big and noticeable objects rather than small or perceptually less accessible ones. Correspondently, the words used to represent for those easily conceptualized are preferably picked up and regarded as unmarked by language speakers opposed to the marked ones. Naturally the time span allotted to process the unmarked words is less than the time period spent to the access of the marked item which is always encoded as marked words by speakers. It further verifies that the positive-negative order in some coordinate idioms is not arbitrary, but motivated.

When describing the up-down and front-back dimensions, Lyons (1979) explicates that the two of asymmetrical pairs are simultaneously characterized in polarity:

> "What is above the ground and in front of us is, characteristically, visible to us and is available for interaction; what is beneath the ground or behind us, is not. Upwards and frontwards are positive, whereas downwards and backwards are negative, in an egocentric perceptual and interactional space based on the notions of visibility and confrontation." (p. 691)

It is agreed in the study that Lyons' explanation of asymmetrical pairs of dimension can be categorized into the positive-negative order. However, the proposal in this respect is that the polarity belongs to the markedness principle because those negative feelings are always characteristic of markedness, containing extraordinary or additional reasons or information.

Lyons' ignorance of right-left dimension is due to the cognitive fact that right-left direction is symmetrical and neither side is more salient than the other. Thus there are no or rather weak criteria for recognizing the right-hand side as positive and the left-hand side as negative.

In regard to distinguishing the positive from the negative, the concepts of "*long*", "*wide*", and "*high*" among the concept pairs such as "*long and short*", "*wide and narrow*", "*high and low*" and so forth, tend to be applied to express linear measurement positively because their indefinite extensions can conceptually indicate the abilities, powers and strengths, while their counterparts conceptually contain the negative connotations of inabilities, shortness and weakness. Therefore, the concepts concerning "*short*", "*narrow*", "*low*" lie in the polarity of being negative, and are less preferable and less used by people. Sentences below are good illustrations to support this attitude.

(68) a. How long is the stick?

a' * How short is the stick?

b. How high is the tower?

b' * How low is the tower?

c. How deep is the water?

c' * How shallow is the water?

d. How big is the bear?

d. * How small is the bear?

In the average interrogatives shown in examples (68a), (68b), (68c) and (68d), the English usage tendency that adjectives such as "*long*", "*high*", "*deep*", and "*big*" are preferably applied to when a question is raised referring to length, height, depth as well as width in denoting a diversity of spatial dimensions because they are conceptually considered as positive or at least neutral extension in space. By contrast, their counterparts are avoided or unacceptable in the interrogatives because they lack the conceptual denotations of positive extension of length, height, depth, width, and size in man's conceptual processing.

If what Greenberg (1966) points out is true that in any language the positive word is always the unmarked one, while the negative is marked one, in compounds composed of a pair of opposites, the propensity of ordering "*positive before negative*" accordingly is included into the principle of the unmarked-marked order (Chao 1968: 139). In the case of coordinate idioms, the pairs involved in this propensity can be generally categorized as follows:

(69) a. Measurement: wide and narrow; tall and short; long and short; high and low; deep and shallow; thick and thin

b. Quantity: big and small; many (much) and few (little); fat and thin; more or less; heavy and light; most and least

c. Quality: good and evil; good and bad; good and poor; rich and poor; the haves and have-nots; friend or foe; for and against; accept or deny; for better or worse; happy or unhappy; assert or deny; yes or no; plus or minus; like and dislike; true or false; three dos and three don'ts;

right and wrong; profit and loss; through fair and foul; weal and woe; all or none

d. Others: strong or weak; fast or slow; beautiful or ugly; true or false; move or stay; hot or cold/difficult or easy; far or near

However, the adjective "*difficult*" in the coordinate construction "*difficult and easy*" and the adjective "*far*" in that of "*far and near*" are placed initially though they are logically negative. Unlike the adjective opposites such as "*deep and shallow*", "*long and short*" and "*tall and shor*t", which profile the factual stretch that can be easily and physically perceived by human beings, the concepts symbolized in the adjectives "*difficult*" and "*far*" are never processed concretely. The recognization of these words is often undergone through the principle which holds the cognitively salient characteristic and which draws more attention of humans. A cognitively positive item, comparably, possesses more salient characteristics than a cognitively negative one. As far as the adjectives "*difficult*" and "*far*" are concerned, they have more salient characteristics than the corresponding adjective "*easy*" and "*near*" in accomplishing a task or a walk through the road, seemingly because the mental disadvantages of coping with an activity draw more attention than the advantages do. The mental cognizing of the concept "*far*" is more prominent than the processing of the adjective "*near*" as the long distance needs more mental conceptualization than that of the short distance. For this reason the former is more sensitive than the latter in language practice. The Chinese equivalent expressions identically accord with the positive-negative order.

(70) a. Measurement: 宽窄 (wide and narrow); 高矮 (tall and short); 长短 (long and short); 高低 (high and low); 深浅 (deep and shallow); 厚薄 (thick and thin)

b. Quantity: 大小 (big and small); 多少 (many and few; much and little); 胖瘦 (fat and thin)/ 轻重 (* light and heavy)

c. Quality: 善恶 (good and evil); 优劣 (good and poor); 好坏 (good and bad); 好坏 (for better or worse); 幸与不幸 (happy or unhappy); 确准与否 (assert or deny); 是否 (yes or no)；加减（plus or minus)；好恶（like and dislike)；真假（true or false)；三要三不要（three dos and three don'ts)；对错（right or wrong)；盈亏（profit and loss)；好运厄运（through fair and foul)；有无（all or none)；敌友（foe or friend）/祸福（weal and woe/ * woe and weal)；贫富（rich and poor/ * poor and rich)；穷人富人(haves and have-nots/ * have-nots and haves)

d. Others：多少（more or less)；快慢（fast or slow)；美丑(beautiful or ugly)；正误（true or false)；动静（move or stay)/难易（difficult or easy)；远近（far or near)

Except for the coordinate constructions like "*rich and poor*", "*weal and woe*" and "*haves and have-nots*", every other Chinese expression maps into its English equivalent, surprisingly the ones "*difficult and easy*" and "*far and near*" included. It satisfies the foregoing explanation concerning cognitive saliency choice of positive-negative order in both expressions "*difficult and easy*" and "*far and near*". The property of positive-negative order in this case, has been seen to be a principle of arranging the coordinate idioms in both English and Chinese.

However, there is now another point to which we need to pay heed to. In Chinese, the word choices of "*poor*" and "*have-nots*" preceding the ones "*rich*" and "*haves*" can be provided as the evidence against the positive-negative order in coordinate idioms. Unfortunately, they cannot be explained by other principles. In fact, I am continually struck by such phenomena, not only in the two selected languages, but in other languages like Korean or Japanese. The fact leads to the belief that though quite a number of coordinate idioms are affected by cognitive or iconic factors, there are still exceptions which will point to the opposite preferences①. Despite this, we are convinced by a majority of the data that the rigidly fixed order in coordinate idioms is not arbitrary. In the meanwhile, a reverse order arrangement can be also found in some Chinese con-

① I now believe that tackling all the problems in fixed expressions could be involved in various issues. Thus in the present study I just report my preliminary findings on the interesting topic and I hope that a fairly explicit theory for the coordinate constructions will be culminated in the near future.

structions which are listed in example (71):

(71)悲喜(happiness and sadness / * sadness and happiness);
祸福(weal and woe/ * woe and weal);
强弱 (weak and strong/ * strong and weak);
轻重(heavy and light/ * light and heavy)

It is seen in example (71) that in Chinese the coordinate idiom "祸福" is a reverse of the positive-negative order. It is thought to be originated from the traditional Chinese Confucian thoughts. When the bad fortune comes, one needs not to feel depressed because it entails the forthcoming fortune. And when the fortune finally comes, one should not be overexcited because it also harbors the bad fortunes. Conventionally speaking, the concept "祸" is characterized as much more salient than the concept "福"entailed in Chinese traditional culture. This can be a good case of conventional saliency. The explanation from conventional saliency has the power on the Chinese coordinate idioms like"悲喜"and"轻重".

4. 5. Discussion and summary

The efforts to analyze the sequential rules of both English and Chinese coordinate constructions can support the fact that their orders are not arbitrarily arranged, neither are they arbitrarily fixed. Instead, their ordering accords with the cognitive conceptualization of processing the meanings of the coordinate constructions when the two constituents within the construction have to be placed in certain sequence. The findings of the analysis further prove the compatibility with the goal of this research that iconicity principles can account for word order phenomena at the phrasal level.

On account of the arrangement principles of coordinate constructions via substantial English and Chinese data, the conclusion is drawn that both Chinese and English coordinate constructions are to a considerable extent iconic of the temporal sequence of the event occurrence when they happen in the real world (i. e. the order of natural phenomena, the order of human experiential activities or the cause-effect/condition-result order) and the spatial order when things occur in reality (i. e. the egocentric, vertical and horizontal order in space). Depending on human conceptual experiences, it is also found that these spatial orders are on a prominence degree: vertical directionality is physically and psychologically the most salient of the spatial dimensions; horizontal dimension has a great impact on the linear ordering concept, ranking as the salient spatial dimension; but right-left order is the least salient because of its symmetricity.

That many similarities in the two languages are found and successfully explained can further verify that though frozen pairs of both languages are said to be theoretically arbitrary, their apparently superficial order similarity cannot lead people to neglecting the fact that their orders are intrinsically governed or mostly iconically motivated by some principles.

The viewpoint of handling coordinate constructions in light of the unmarked-marked order and positive-negative order from an iconic perspective is rather a new one. It is in agreement with Lyons'(1979: 691) observation:

"It has been plausibly argued that polarity and markedness in pairs of directional opposites derive not only in the vocabulary of location and locomotion, but more generally, from the natural properties of the egocentric perceptual space and the spatial orientation and physical asymmetries of the human body."

Lyons means here that the polarity and markedness orders are essentially motivated by human perceptual and physical experiences. Furthermore, the unmarked-marked order principle proposed in the present study further testifies that Birdsong's (1995) assumption that "the respective roles of markedness, cognitive constraints and iconicity are considered as independent or exclusive of one another", is not necessarily the case. On the contrary, the research results manifest that whether it is marked or positive, it is conceptually-oriented marked or positive and is intentionally made in the salient position in linguistic representations. Therefore, either markedness principle or cognitive constraint can be incorporated into iconicity in that it is very obviously shown in both English and Chinese coordinate constructions that the orders of most coordinate expression influenced by both markedness principle and cognitive constraints follow human perceptual or conceptual structures. It is definitely applicable to the sequential order principle: the linear sequence of linguistic structures iconically corresponds to the conceptual order it represents.

Despite of the fact that there are a handful of exceptions that violate the rules when the coordinate constructions in both English and Chinese have to be sequenced, they can fortunately be explained phonologically, historically or conventionally. The results of the study profoundly find that the amount of exceptional examples in Chinese is greater than those in English. Most Chinese expressions reversed to the constituent order that need to be obeyed in coordinate idioms are in the end able to be explained by referring to deep-seated conventions of Chinese cultures. The distinction pervasively leads to the fact that the linguistic phenomenon of Chinese coordinate constructions is a much more culture-dependent language compared to that in English. Opposite to it, the order of English coordinate expressions, mostly consistently iconic of conceptual structures, indicates that in the domain of coordinate constructions, English is a language which favorably corresponds to the experiential world. Given the wide range of material to be considered, it would be impossible to exhaust the topic at hand, but an attempt has been made to present some main features of cognitive linguistic theorizing with reference to the semantic explanation of the ordering of constituents within both English and Chinese coordinate constructions. However, it should be pointed out that owing to the limited data supplied here, this point may bear some problems in terms of explanatory adequacy because of its inability to completely predict all the phenomena in coordinate constructions.

CHAPTER FIVE　AN ICONIC ANALYSIS OF WORD ORDER WITHIN PRENOMINAL MODIFIERS

Ungerer and Schmid (2008) in their explanation of iconicity used the examples of how the prenominal modifiers within an English noun phrase to postulate the existence of linear sequence of elements within a linguistic expression that are integrated on the ground of the characteristics embodied in the real world. When different word order possibilities of prenominal modifiers within a noun phrase are taken into consideration, it becomes immediately obvious that many word order phenomena are associated with the iconicity principles, which is going to be discussed in this chapter. The relevant study in this research will attach focus on three research questions given as follows:

1) Can the distance principle of iconicity be considered as an external motivation for prenominal modifier ordering? And what are the possible rules related to the distance principle?

2) If distance principle is able to be seen as its external motivator to sequence prenominal modifiers, what maxims need to be followed?

3) What is the cognitive mechanism that motivates the sequential order of prenominal determiners and modifiers?

The first section of this chapter introduces and distinguishes between the two types of modifiers: prenominal modifiers and post-nominal modifiers. The second section goes into details about the explanation of ordering within the determiners which are considered as a type of prenominal modifiers. Section three is devoted to the explanation of the sequencing of multiple determiners employed to be modifiers in front of the head noun. Section four will briefly mention the order among prenominal adjectives when functioning as modifiers.

5. 1. Definitions of modifiers within an English noun phrase

The linguists have treated various aspects of modifiers from a diversity of theoretical sources. According to them, a modifier is defined as a medium to expand the basic grammatical structure to complicated information chunk. Chao (1968: 274) defines a modifier within a noun phrase as "an expression X is said to modify an expression Y when XY is an endocentric construction and Y, but not X, is the centre. X is called the attribute or modifier, and Y the head or the modified part." That is to say, a modifier is generally seen as a constituent in an endocentric construction, which imparts information to the head of the construction. The referent of the head within a noun phrase can be identified with the information that its modifier gives. It can be exemplified as:

(72) a. *the very hot* soup

b. *a tall*, *handsome* stranger

In example (72a), the constituents "*the*" and "*very hot*" are respectively the modifiers and deliver specific information to the endocentric construction "*the very hot soup*", in which the noun "*soup*" is the head noun. And within the noun phrase "*a tall handsome stranger*" in example (72b), the elements "*a*", "*tall*" and "*handsome*" are identically modifiers which help audience easily identify the entity designated within the noun phrase. That is what the head noun "*stranger*" is referring to.

Viewed from traditional structural grammar and Generative Grammar, the structure description of a noun phrase aligned with prenominal modifiers can be given in diagram shown in (73):

(73) NP → (DET) (AP) N

DET → the, a, an, this, that, my, Tom's ...

AP → interesting, big, very brave...

N → apple, idea, car, table...

Taylor (1996: 97) claims that "both nouns and noun phrases designate things, on Langacker's schematic① definition of things. The difference is that whereas a noun (an N or N') designates a kind, or type of thing, a noun phrase designates an instance of the kind (or instances, in case the noun phrase is plural)." For instance, the noun "*bus*" belongs to a kind of genus that is classified as a transportation means, while the noun phrase "*a new sleeping bus*" merely refers to a specific one in the type of transportation means.

Cognitive Linguistics views nouns as the process of providing ground for noun phrases. Grounding implies a relation between the designated instance and the ground, i. e. the circumstances of the speech situation, and the participants that are involved in it. Its two aspects involved here are: some notions of number or quality conveyed by the noun, and some process of grounding. Some nominals with definite reference convey that the instance can be uniquely identified by both speaker and hearer, while those with non-specific reference pick out an instance (or instances) that cannot be definitely

① Langacker (1987b:371) defines a schema as an abstract characterization that is fully compatible with all the members of the category it defines[…] it is an integrated structure that embodies the commonality of its members, which are conceptions of greater specificity and detail that elaborate the schema in contrasting ways.

recognized. Take the above-mentioned noun for example once more. The noun "*bus*", though it designated a kind of transportation means (i. e. school bus, mini bus, city bus, new bus, old bus ... etc.) provides a good grounding for the noun phrase "*a new sleeping bus*" because it can be quite naturally regarded as a specific instance within the domain of the entities existing in the physical world, referred to in a nominal form of "*bus*".

5. 2. Classifications of modifiers

Although the study on modifiers has been fruitful over the century, both the classifications and the semantic identifications of modifiers in either English or Chinese are by no means an easy issue to tackle. Take the positions of modifiers within a noun phrase into consideration. It is upon recent years that linguists come into an agreement that there are mainly two types of modifiers in terms of their respective positions with respect to the head noun: prenominal and post-nominal modifiers. The following table can clearly show their distinctions.

Table 2. Two types of modifiers within an English noun phrase

Prenominal modifiers	Head noun	Post-nominal modifiers
a good	book	
my	family	
car	widow	
women's	magazine	
smiling	face	
the	president	*of the university*
the	time	*to go to school*
the	girl	*standing near the door*

续表

Prenominal modifiers	Head noun	Post-nominal modifiers
five	sons	*who have died gloriously*
our	friends	*abroad*

It is seen from table 2, modifiers within an English noun phrase can be placed either in front of or at back of the head noun; they are therefore categorized as prenominal modifiers and post-nominal modifiers. Prenominal modifiers are the constituents that usually take the positions preceding the head noun to identify more information to the head noun. The examples in table 2 in the meantime show that by "prenominal modifiers", what can be included into the category are such linguistic elements as determiners①, adjectives, as well as nouns. Besides, prenominal modifiers can be realized by adjectivals. By "adjectival", Kim believes that all kind of constituents that can satisfy an adjective grammar function, so to speak, including a noun phrase, (past/present) participles, gerunds and sometimes via phrases. They can be exemplified as in (74) below:

(74) a. his life story; an iron rod; assembly lines; a gold watch; flower garden

b. a dull English book; the light green waves; decent young people; fast food

c. a drunken man; a rotten apple; sunken eyes; a retired teacher

d. running shoes; boiling point; swimming pool; dining room

e. a come-and-fight-me attitude; round-the-clock service; an up-to-date timetable; happily-married couples

① Some researchers believe determiners, such as possessives, demonstratives, numerals, articles and quantifiers, etc. to be exclusive of the category of prenominal modifiers. However, in the study, determiners are categorized into its group because it is found while observing the data, that determiners also follow the sequential rules in the process of constituent arrangement.

All the examples seen in (74) indicate that prenominal modifiers in English can be identified by a wide range of constituents varying from nouns, adjectives, participles, gerunds to phrases. It is also shown more than one modifier can be co-existent within a noun phrase if only they can find their proper positions and are ordered appropriately within the phrase (e. g. *a dull English book*, *the light green waves*). More examples can be given below.

(75) a. an unwelcome state guest/ * state unwelcome guest

b. an established historical fact/ * a historical established fact

c. some interesting valuable facts/ ? valuable interesting facts

(76) a. a sensational new screen find/ * a new screen sensational find

b. a popular wartime propaganda film/ * a popular propaganda wartime film

c. those indelible red lip marks/ * those red lip indelible marks

It is observed from examples (75) and (76) that when two or more prenominal modifiers co-occur within an English noun phrase, they are seemingly subject to a fixed sequence, which cannot be arbitrarily reversed. What is the order principle that they need to follow? And what is the motivation behind it? The task of this chapter is to unveil the possible motivated mechanism behind the preferred order regularity of these prenominal modifiers.

Unlike prenominal modifiers, post-nominal modifiers are the constituents that are uniformly placed after the head noun. They are largely represented by adjectives, adverbs, (present or past) participles, (prepositional) phrases, small clauses or the subordinate clauses. The examples are given in (77) below:

(77) a. a tile falling from a roof; the girl giving such an intelligent answer

b. the car repaired by the mechanic; food eaten for today; dog awakened by the noise

c. the man to help you; the place to stay; the difficulties to overcome; letters to write

d. the road to Glasgow; this book on grammar; the tree by the river

e. the fastest car imaginable; the only food tolerable; all events remarkable

f. somcthing new; God almighty; the house ablaze; anything interesting

g. the only girl who can play the guitar; the driveway which had been set on fire; a student who studies Physics at Cambridge University

Experts say that post-nominal modifiers are mostly characteristic of eventuality. Therefore they exhibit a much more complicated syntactic form and a more sophisticated representative meaning. No wonder such constituents as prepositional phrases, finite or non-finite clauses can function in a large part as post-nominal rather than prenominal modifiers. This reason gives an impetus to scrutinize merely the ordering of the prenominal modifiers in the present research, leaving post-nominal modifier arrangement for later study topic.

In their paper "Prenominal Adjective Ordering in English and Mandarin", Sproat and Shin (1988) predict that there is a cognitive basis for the ordering restriction conditions of prenominal modifications. Unfortunately, they could not, at that time, supply their study with a powerful explanation for the relationship between the cognitive basis of the ordering and the effect it has upon the grammar (1988: 487). Later on, Ungerer and Schmid (1996: 253) take into an account of ordering the prenominal modifiers appealing to the distance principle of iconicity theory, although they failed to conduct follow-up studies to provide strong evidence to verify what kinds of modifiers are conceptually attracted by the head, or what linguistic or semantic criteria can be relied on to distinguish the close from the distant correlations between modifiers and the head.

The aim in this chapter is not to argue against the viewpoint from Ungerer and Schmid but attempts to extend it by implementing the respective semantic properties of prenominal modifiers and the head noun they are designated to modify. Thus a possible investigation into the pre-linguistic evidence from the iconic perspective to identify what semantic features a head noun and its modifiers can have in order for them to stay closer

will be achieved.

When different word order possibilities within a noun phrase are taken into consideration, it becomes immediately obvious that prenominal modifiers are always the center of study. However, it is not only primarily reflected in the placements of the modifiers, such as nouns, adjectives, present or past participles, but also the position relation of determiners positioned before a head noun, which are argued to be a type of prenominal modifiers in this study. Included in the category are necessarily the generic quantifiers, identifying determiners and numerals. The aim in the following section is to explore the sequential distance of determiners within a noun phrase.

5.3. Linear order of determiners

Bolinger (1981: 69) defines determiners as "[are] used relatively more often than lexical words to point elements in language or to the roles of speakers and hearers, and less often to point to things and events in the real world." Determiners, noted by Bolinger (1981) as functional words, cannot be omitted in most situations and execute the syntactic functions more than the semantic coherences with the head noun.

Modifiers are usually optional because they only add the conceptual information to the head noun and the omission of a modifier may not lead to a conceptual incoherence but to an impoverishment of semantic structures. Contrary to the modifiers, determiners within a noun phrase are special and indispensable elements, which display the exterior features of the head noun or only relate the state of the head to its environment. Therefore they take the position different from that of the prenominal modifiers because they play distinctive roles within the noun phrase. In other words, determiners do not influence the semantic concepts of the head noun. They indicate instead the features exterior to the head noun by either counting their quantities, identified as the *quantifiers* like "*some*", "*all*", "*three*", "*half*", etc. or identifying their correlations with the contextual background, symbolized as *definite articles*, *possessives and demonstratives.* In conclusion, determiners include definite and indefinite articles, like the linguistic symbols "*the*", "*a*" or "*an*"; possessives such as "*my*, *your*, *his*, *her*, *our*, *my mother's*, *our teachers'*, *the nation's*, *Mary's*, etc."; numerals given in the forms "*six*, *forty*, *twenty*, *first*, etc."; demonstratives, for instance "*this*, *that*, *these*, *those*, *etc.*" and other determiners involving what are traditionally called quantifiers like "*some*, *many*, *few*, *all*, *half*, *every*, *another*" and so on. Let us take the sentence "*I drunk the cold coffee.*" for example.

(78) a. I drunk <the> <cold> coffee.

b. I drunk <the> coffee.

c. I drunk <cold> coffee.

Sentence (78b) is no less coherent than sentence (78a) for the reason that the definite article "*the*" in the noun phrase "*the coffee*" is an element employed to establish mental contact with discourse space (Langacker 1991a: 98) similar to the phrase "*the cold coffee*" in (78a). Contrary to the situation, the lack of the article "*the*" in sentence (78c) makes the sentence conceptually incoherent or utterly isolated from the communicative context, consequently hard to decode by speaker and listener, though grammatically acceptable.

It thus can be concluded that determiners are different from modifiers in terms of the different features they carry. Modifiers denote the features parasitic to the head noun, thus they are sometimes optional, while determiners embody the features self-contained to the head but relating to the context or the background, thus they are mostly obligatory. Further examples are shown in (79):

(79) a. < those/five > < sweet > potatoes

b. < our > < convention > site

c. < a > < leaky > roof

What can be summarized in example (79) is that the modifiers "*sweet*" in example (79a), "*convention*" in example (79b) and "*leaky*" in example (79c) containing the intrinsic semantic concepts of their noun phrases, are placed closer to the head, while the determiners "*those*", "*five*", "*our*" and "*a*" used respectively in examples (79a), (79b) and (79c), precede those modifier because they denote the features extrinsic to the head noun either serving a referential function (i. e. the determiners used to refer to the definite and specific like "my", "the", "these" and "those") or indefinite and non – specific entities, or a quantifying function (i. e. the determiners used to specify the numbers of the entities, such as *some*, *any or five*). Therefore, the rule of ordering determiners and other modifiers can be generalized into:

(80) The principle of ordering determiners and modifiers:

Modifiers are always placed closer to the head than determiners because modifiers conceptually share the intrinsic semantic features of the head, while determiners only carry the features extrinsic to the head or the features apt to relate the head to the communicative context.

However, we find, in most cases, more than one determiner occurs simultaneously within a noun phrase, in particular when they bear different syntactic functions. Next comes the problem of how determiners can be arranged into a good order. Traditional studies (Langacker 1987) categorize determiners into two: determiners with identifying functions and those with quantifying functions like the following examples:

(81) a. < these > < three > (black) cats/ * < three > < these > (black) cats

b. < the > only < one > child/ * < one > < the > only child

Unfortunately, we observed that in some cases, more than two determiners co-occur within a noun phrase, as shown in (82) below.

(82) a. all those three tables / * those all three tables

In example (82), quantifiers like "all" and "three" are all determiners signaling the quantities, they are placed differently in a noun phrase. Thus it is argued that quantifying determiners could be further divided. Furthermore it is found that the reason for the linear order of determiners within a noun phrase fails to be elaborated in former studies. This study intends to introduce Distance Principle of Iconicity as an explanatory key to the present problem. A motivation hypothesis for the order of determiners within a noun phrase can be formed which predicts that in the process of ordering determiners, the close position to the head noun will be indicated by the close concepts between the two elements; the distant position to the head will be indicated by the possibility that the two elements do not have close concepts.

According to the original categorization, it is said that the identifying determiners always precede the determiners serving a quantifying functions. For example:

(83) a. < these > < three > (black) cats/ * < three > < these > (black) cats
b. < the > only < one > child/ * < one > < the > only child
c. < my > < two > (doting) "mothers"/ * < two > < my > (doting) "mothers"

Naturally, under no circumstances can the determiners reverse the positions with modifiers. It seems clear that the modifiers "*black*" and "*doting*" in (83a) and (83c), denoting the intrinsic semantic concepts of their noun phrases, are placed closer to the head nouns, while the determiners serving a quantifying functions (i. e. the quantifying determiner, *three* in (83a), *one* in (83b) and *two* in (83c)), or signaling a referential function (i. e. the identifying determiners, like demonstrative "*these*" in (83a), definite article "*the*" in (83b), and possessive "*my*" in (83c)), are less close to the head noun. To put it another way, those determiners, having identifying or quantifying functions, are conceptually and formally more distant from the head noun than the modifiers having qualifying function (i. e. denoting intrinsic features of the head).

We also observe that the determiners serving the quantifying functions always precede the determiners signaling a referential function. When this is linked to the conceptual distance principle of iconicity, the relative order of the identifying and quantifying determiners within a noun phrase can be stated as follows:

(84) a. The more quantifying features prenominal modifiers of an NP have, the closer they are to the head noun.

b. The more identifying features prenominal modifiers of an NP have, the more distant they are to the head noun.

Under this claim, we can decide the linear order among quantifying determiners, identifying determiners and other modifiers within a noun phrase in terms of their functions, shown as follows:

(85) The linear order of premodifiers within an NP:

Identifying Determiners > Quantifying Determiners > other modifiers > the HEAD noun

Unfortunately, it is further observed that in some cases, more than two determiners co-exist within a noun phrase as shown in example (86) and (87).

(86) a. those tables /three tables

b. those *three* tables/ * *three those* tables

c. *all those three* tables / * *those all three* tables/ * *three those all* tables

(87) a. my friends /two friends

b. *my two* friends/ * *two my* friends

c. *both my two* friends / * *two my both* friends/ * *my two both* friends

It is of interest to note that in (86a) and (87a) it is possible to refer to a noun phrase either by identifying the entity or by quantifying the entity. When we consider the order of determiners in front of the head noun, those determiners specifying the numbers are closer to the head noun than those containing an identifying function, as shown in (86b) and (87c). What is seen in (86c) and (87c) is that when those determiners with generic quantity are involved, they precede the determiners with the identifying functions. Hence the order of determiners within a noun phrase is like this: quantifiers with generic interpretation precede the identifying determiners, which in turn come before those quantifiers with numeral specification.

Thus it is proposed here that the determiners having quantifying function should be divided into two types: the quantifying determiner with its number specific and the quantifying determiner with its number non-specific. The former will be defined in this article as numerals, indicating those determiners which can quantitatively specify the interpretations of numbers, such as "*six*, *two*, *one*, etc". The latter is defined as generic quantifiers, referring to those determiners which cannot quantitatively specify the interpretations of numbers, such as "*some*, *few*, *all*, *many*, etc". At this point, the order among determiners within a noun phrase is generalized as below:

(88) The order among determiners within a noun phrase:

Generic quantifiers > identifying determiners > numerals > the HEAD noun

One further question to ask, under this circumstance, is: why will generic quantifiers come off before the identifying determiners, while numerals go after them instead?

Observe the noun phrases in (89) and (90) that include determiners.

(89) a. the/ten good books

b. all the ten good books

c. all the good books

d. * all ten good books

(90) a. my/two friends

b. both my two friends

c. both my friends

d. * both two friends

It is seen from (89a) and (90a) that a noun phrase can be modified by either identifying determiners (i. e. *the* and *my*) or by numerals (i. e. *ten* and *two*). When generic quantifiers like *all* and *both* appear, they can exist either along together with both identifying determiners and numerals as in (89b) and (90b), or only with the identifying determiners as in (89c) and (90c). However, the noun phrases would be ungrammatical when generic quantifiers can co-exist with numerals separate from identifying determiners, like (89d) and (90d).

Huddleston (1984: 233) has claimed that "a noun phrase may contain up to three determiners: '*all her many* ideas...' ". Unfortunately, when generic quantifiers and numerals co-exist in front of the head noun, the noun phrase is proved to be unacceptable. In this context, I would refer to Kim's (2007b) observation that goes like this:

> There is no noun phrase in English which contains more than one determiner, except when a definite determiner such as *the*, *this*, *his*, etc. is preceded by multipliers such as *double*, *three times*, etc.; determiners marking faction such as *one-third*, etc.; determiners marking totality such as *all* and *both*; or indefinite determiners marking quantity such as *some*, *most*, etc.

What is implied in his remarks is that in order to construct multiple determiners within a noun phrase, generic quantifiers like multipliers can only survive on the condition that an identifying determiner (other than numerals) is present. In other words, generic quantifiers like multipliers are actually dependent on or inseparable from the identifying determiners. The exact fact of generic quantifiers' dependence on the identifying determiners limits the generic quantifiers to go straightforward the identifying determiners and keep close to each other.

To continue, in the condition of generic quantifiers, we need a deeper explanations because certain generic quantifiers cannot directly precede the identifying determiners unless a preposition "*of*" is inserted between two elements, as exemplified below in phrases (91a) and (91b).

(91) a. some/most of his friends

b. * some/most his friends

The above mentioned phenomena can be named as "of-insertion". It is motivated by partitive constructions (i. e., 'X of Y', implying that X is (a) part of the whole Y) to prevent the use of illegally combined determiners as in (91b), but to allow the use of *some of the/his* as in (91a). However, not all the cases in generic quantifiers necessitate the presence of the "of-insertion". Some exceptions can be found, too. Exceptions are seen in phrases (92).

(92) a. * double of the price /double the price

b. both of my sisters /both my sisters

It seems that though equal to the determiners "*some*" and "*most*" shown in (91), functioning as generic modifiers, the determiners "*double*" in (92a) and "*both*" in (92b) are either impossible or optional to be inserted by the preposition "*of*" between two determiners. The description of *of*-insertion reveals that the linguistic distance of some generic quantifiers are greater from the head noun than the others.

Kim (2007b) argues that all the cases, in effect, can be treated in relation to the optionality of the preposition "of" in "of-insertion". He suggests adopting a partitive construction and a mathematic perspective to view the "of-insertion" problem.

Viewed from the mathematic perspective, notions such as totality, multiplication and fraction might be a single one such as 'multiplication' or in a broad sense 'X'. We convert linguistic signs into mathematic signs as follows:

(93) (1) a. all the five: 5 ′× 1′

b. both the (two): 2 ′× 1′

(2) a. double the (Y): 2 ′× (Y) ′

b. three times the (Y): 3′ × (Y) ′

(3) a. half the (Y): (Y) ′× 1/2′

b. two-thirds the (Y): (Y) ′× 2/3′

The so-called generic quantifiers like *all*, *double*, *one-third*, etc. function to total, widen or narrow the scope or range of the given amount or numbers referred to by those generic quantifiers.

Kim (2007b) also presents three conditions for the "*of*-insertion" to license determiner combinations given as follows:

(94) (1) "Of is optional when [X = Y]"

a. all (of) the/his books (e. g. if Y is 20, then X is 20)

X Y

b. both (of) these/my friends (e. g. if Y is 2, then X is 2)

(2) "Of is obligatory when [X < Y]"

a. some/many of the/his friends? (e. g. if Y is 6, then X is less than 6)

X Y

b. much/little of the/this milk (e. g. if Y is 6 litre, then X is less than 6)

(3) "The of-insertion is impossible when [X > Y], because of its violation"

e. g. double/twice the/this price? (e. g. if Y is $5, then X is $10)

X Y

However, we can see that certain examples will violate these conditions, as shown below in the example (95). Both quantifiers "h*alf*" and "*one-third*" are optional though they belong to condition (2), referring to part of the whole.

(95) a. half (of) the/these/my friends

b. one-third (of) the earth

The use of generic quantifiers together with the preposition "*of*" in (95a) and (95b) is explainable because the X (i. e *half* and *one-third*) refers to (a) part of Y. But the problem surely arises when the quantifiers "*half*" and "*one-third*" occur without the preposition "*of*". They falsify the condition (3) in (94). Kim explains it by stating that because the quantifiers "*half/one-third*", as a faction, can be multiplied (i. e. 1/2 X (friends)'and 1/3 X (earth)') by another number, they can be followed by another determiner without the preposition "*of*" in between. Thus Kim's three conditions can be revised as follows:

(96) (1) "Of is optional when [X ≦ Y] and X can be multiplied by Y."

a. all (of) the/his books (e. g. if Y is 20, then X is 20)

X Y

b. both (of) these/my friends (e. g. if Y is 2, then X is 2)

X Y

c. half (of) the/these/my friends (e. g. if Y is 20, then X is 10)

X Y

d. one-third (of) the earth (e. g. if Y is 120, then X is 40)

(2) "Of is obligatory when [X < Y] and X cannot be multiplied by Y."

a. some/many of the/his friends (e. g. if Y is 6, then X is less than 6)

X Y

b. much/little of the/this milk (e. g. if Y is 6 liter, then X is less than 6)

(3) "Of-insertion is impossible when [X > Y] because of its violation."

a. double/twice the/this price (e. g. if Y is $5, then X is $10)

X Y

The three conditions concerning the "*of*-insertion" construction clearly explain the difference of the combinations between generic quantifiers. It is because of the insertion of the preposition "*of*" that the linguistic distance of different groups of generic quantifiers to the head noun can be interpreted in terms of the distance principle of iconicity. The following examples can show it clearly.

(97)	(most distant)	< some/most of his friends >/ * some/most his friend
		< all/both (of) my sisters >
	↓	
	(closest)	< double/twice the price >/ * double/twice of the price

The generic quantifiers show a hierarchy of distance towards the HEAD noun. If the preposition "of" is obligatory, the generic quantifier is least close to the HEAD noun; If the preposition "of" is optional, the generic quantifier is less close; If the preposition "of" is impossible, the generic quantifier is closest to the HEAD. The explanation to the distance of generic quantifiers can be shown in Table 3.

Table 3: The distance of generic quantifiers from the HEAD noun

CONDITIONS FOR "OF" INSERTION	GENERIC QUANTIFIERS	"OF" INSERTION	HEAD NOUN	DISTANCE TO HEAD
a. X < Y b. X cannot be multiplied by Y	*some/many/most/few/much/little...*	obligatory "of"	his friends	close
a. X ≦ Y b. X can be multiplied by Y	*all/both/each...* (*additions: half/one-third*)	optional "of" or "ϕ"	my sisters	closer
X > Y	*double/twice/triple...*	impossible "ϕ"	the price	closest

Suppose the number of the generic quantifier is "X" and "Y" is referred to the total number denoted by the noun phrase, it can be stated as follows:

(98) a. If X is larger than Y, the generic quantifier is closer to the head noun without the insertion of the preposition "*of*".

b. If X is smaller than or equal to Y, and X can be multiplied by Y, the generic quantifier is less close to the head noun with the optional insertion of the preposition "*of*".

c. If X is smaller than Y, but X cannot be multiplied by Y, the generic quantifier is least close to the head noun with the obligatory insertion of the preposition "*of*".

The study of the present section focuses on determiners which are argued to be a type of prenominal modifiers in this investigation. The aim is to explore the sequential distance of determiners within a noun phrase. All the evidence shows that a noun phrase in English can contain maximally three different kinds of determiners which are defined generic quantifiers, identifying determiners and numerals respectively. And based on the distance principle of iconicity, the determiners that are conceptually nearer to the HEAD will stay closer to it. Thus the order among determiners within a noun phrase is concluded as: generic quantifiers > identifying determiners > numerals > the HEAD noun. It proves that the distance principle of iconicity has a great explanatory power to prenominal modifiers ordering.

5.4. Linear order of adjectivals as prenominal modifiers

After the orders of determiners are examined, research emphasis needs to be laid on the ordering of the constituents within a noun phrase going after all the three types of determiners. The examples provided in (99) illustrate that the constituents going after the determiners are in most part adjectival.

(99) a. the two lucky students

b. all the running cars

c. some established historical fact

In addition to the determiners, most of the modifiers are attributed to the constituents that can function as adjectives to modify a HEAD noun. They include adjectives, gerunds, (present or past) participles, nouns or noun phrases. To account for the rules of ordering this type of prenominal modifiers, its literature views have to be first of all taken look at.

The ordering among all the adjectivals as prenominal modifiers① is such an important issue in foreign language learning because it greatly affects the fluency of language.

① The order of prenominal modifiers of this type discussed in this section include all those that are canonical or in the preferred order, while those of irregular ordering of prenominal modifiers are exclusive in this section.

In the process of generating complex clauses, there often occur the situations in which a series of constituents get clustered to modify a single HEAD noun. For instance, both the nominal phrases "*large foreign financial firms*" and "*zero-coupon global bonds*" are acceptable, while their counterparts "*foreign large financial firms*" and "*global zero-coupon bonds*" sound odd. It seems that there must exist certain structural principles to be observed by the modifiers when they have to stay within a phrase. However, the difficulties in specifying a consistent ordering of adjectival as prenominal modifiers have already been obviously noted by many linguists (Whorf 1956, Vendler 1968). Given the difficulty of adequately describing all factors that motivate the order of adjectival as prenominal modifiers, most works in literature are based on placing the prenominal modifiers into broad semantic classes, and specifying an order principle among these classes. As early as the year of 1985, Quirk et al (1985: 1341) argue for a subjective-objective gradience determining adjective order such that "modifiers relating to properties which are (relatively) inherent in the head of the noun phrase [...] will tend to be placed nearer to the head and be preceded by modifiers concerned with what is relatively a matter of opinion."

In the meantime, Chinese researchers' painstaking efforts (Zhu 1957, Chao 1968, Gu 1986, Lu 1988, Tai 1988) also give rise to extensive bodies of works that make great contributions to the study of modifier sequence. Zhang (1998) initiates the ordering principle of English adjective modifiers based on classifying the attributes of adjectives. His proposal of the order is given as: general descriptive adjectives > adjectives denoting size/length/height > adjectives denoting shape > adjectives denoting age > adjectives denoting color > adjectives denoting nationality/ provenance/ origin > adjectives related to material > adjectives related to type.

After a careful observation of the data from Chinese and English, it is found that although not exhaustively presented as English classes, the ordering of Chinese adjective modifiers is surprisingly identical to that of English classes. It can be illustrated by the following example. ①

(100) a. the three ①nice ②little ③white ④wooden dolls

a'. 三个 ①漂亮的 ②小 ③白 ④木 娃娃

b. a ①beautiful ②big ③red ball

b'. 一个 ①漂亮的 ②大 ③红球

By comparing the noun phrase given in (100a) and that in (100a'), it can be seen that English and Chinese adjective prenominal modifiers are ordered identically. Looking into the details, both English attribute "*wooden*" and Chinese equivalent "木" can be respectively placed closest to the English HEAD noun "dolls" and Chinese noun "娃娃". Because the English adjective "*white*" and its Chinese correspondence "白" indicate the color of the physical entity and the English adjective "*little*" and its Chinese counterpart "小" belong to the size, thus they are placed next to the modifiers "*wooden*"; "*nice*" and the Chinese adjective "漂亮" are placed more distant from the HEAD noun than the other adjective modifiers. A similar account applies to examples in (100b) and (100b').

The identical order among adjectival prenominal modifiers in the two languages makes one thing certain, and hopefully it is a typological maxim. Behind the formal description exists a commonly shared explanatory motivation to condition the ordering of prenominal modifiers, which deserves a deeper investigation. Consequently, this section is designed to find and explain the related factors influencing the order of adjectival prenominal modifiers by means of the distance principle.

It has been noticed that in addition to adjectives, a group of other constituents can function as adjectival prenominal modifiers, including nouns, gerunds, past and pres-

---

① In this section, the numbers ①②③ and ④ are used to symbolize the natural sequence of the adjectives functioning as prenominal modifiers.

ent participles, among which a particular ordering seems to be invisibly established. Instances of these modifiers are exemplified in (101).

(101) a. a life story (noun)
b. a dining room (gerund)
c. a newly-born baby (past participle)
d. a boring meeting (present participle)
e. the cleverest mouse (descriptive adjective)

All these constituents are involved into the scope of the present study. Many concerns are cast to the motivating factors governing these adjectival prenominal modifiers' distance from the HEAD noun. The discussion in the present part is basically a semantic analysis: what semantic features will affect the distance between various prenominal modifiers and the HEAD noun. Thus it pays attentions to attempt to seek for rules which will govern the order of adjectival prenominal modifiers under the ground of iconicity principle of distance (Haiman 1983, 1985a).

5.4.1. The sequence of adjectives, gerunds and nouns as prenominal modifiers

In English, a sequence of consecutive elements can premodify a HEAD noun, but it is obviously shown that the order of these elements cannot stay randomly nor can they be converted, with examples shown in (102)

(102) a. a long iron rod/ * an iron long rod
b. a newly-designed iron rod/ * an iron newly-designed rod

What can be seen in both example (102a) and (102b) is that the nonimal form "*iron*", functioning as a modifier, is always closest to the HEAD noun "*rod*" either when the descriptive adjective (e. g. "*long*" in (102a)), or the past participle (e. g "*newly-designed*" in (102b)) enters into the noun phrase. The converse is, otherwise, impossible in both cases. What makes the modifier "*iron*" distinctive from descriptive adjective "*long*" and past participle "*newly-designed*"?

According to Haiman's conceptual distance (1983), if concepts are close to one another, they are definitely sharing similar semantic properties, thus linguistically staying close or all together. In employing linguistic and conceptual distance in testing the order of prenominal modifiers, it should be that modifiers linguistically close to the HEAD must be conceptually close to the concept that the noun designated. Again in example (102), the modifier "*iron*" is linguistically and in turn conceptually close to the HEAD noun, which indicates that it might share certain semantic properties that the head noun possesses. Now much concern goes to the semantic features of the noun "*iron*" when it serves as a modifier within a noun phrase. Referring to the semantic explanation from Oxford English-English Dictionary and the English grammar rules, the word "*iron*" here functions in effect as a modifier to describe the quality of a physical entity. Thus it semantically bears the features of being an adjective. Quirk et al (1972) successfully observe four features that are used to distinguish adjectives from others:

(103) a. They freely occur in attribute position. For instance, they can premodify a noun, like the adjective "*happy*" in the noun phrase "*happy children*".

b. They freely occur in predicative position. They can function as subject complement, e. g. the adjective "*old*" in the sentence "*The man seems old.*", or as object complement, e. g. the adjective "*ugly*" in the sentence "*He thought the painting ugly.*"

c. They can be premodified by the intensifier, e. g. the adjective "*happy*" is premodified by intensifier "*very*" in the sentence "*The children are very happy.*"

d. They can take comparative and superlative forms whether inflectionally, e. g. the sentences "*The children are happier now.*" and "*They are the happiest people I know.*" or by the addition of the premodifiers "*more*" and "*most*", like in the sentence "*These students are more intelligent.*" and "*They are the most beautiful paintings I have ever seen.*" (pp. 231 – 232)

Comparing the noun "*iron*" to the other two modifiers (i. e. *long* and *newly-designed*) in light of feature (103b), it is found that the modifier "*iron*" actually shows more nominal characteristics than adjective characteristics, because it occurs only in the object position (e. g *The rod is made of iron*), while the other two modifiers can freely occur in the predicative position (e. g. *The rod is long* and *The rod is newly designed*). Moving to feature (c) given by Quirk et al (1972), it is proved that different from the other two modifiers, the nominal modifier "*iron*" can actually not be premodified by an intensifier (e. g. * *very/more iron*). The comparison clearly shows that the nominal modifier "*iron*", though functioning as a modifier, has more semantic properties of a noun than other modifiers. Intuitively, this is the motivating factor to keep the nominal modifier "*iron*" closest to the HEAD noun. More examples can be given below.

(104) a. a beautiful flower garden/ * a flower beautiful garden

b. an interesting football game/ * a football interesting game

When checking the semantic features of the two modifiers "*flower*" in (104a) and "*football*" in (104b), neither of them can be premodified by any intensifiers (e. g. * *a very flower garden*/ * *a much/very football game*). Nor can they take any comparative or superlative forms except for the fact that they stay in attribute positions and are able to occur in the predicative positions (e. g. "*That is a flower.*" and "*It is a football.*"). That is to say, the two words possess part and parcel of the semantic features of adjective. Thus it can say that when a noun premodifies another noun as HEAD within a noun phrase, it stays closer to the HEAD than adjectives because of their possession of semantic features to certain degree similar to the HEAD.

Besides, it is of great interest to notice that in addition to nouns, gerunds like "*dining*" *in* (105a) and "*running*" in (105b) are competing against noun modifiers for the modifying place that is close to the HEAD noun. Do they have the semantic features equal to nominal modifiers?

(105) a. a new dining room/ * a dining new room

b. a hand-made running shoes/ * a running hand-made shoes

It is seen that gerunds like "*dining*" in (105a) and "*running*" in (105b) tend to stay closer than adjectives to modify the HEAD noun. In light of Quirk et al's observation of the semantic features of an adjective, tests can be used to decide gerunds to be adjectives or not. If changed into relative clauses, gerunds surprisingly occur in the position the same as a prepositional object, which is believed to have a property similar to nouns (e. g. "*The room is for dining.*" and "*The shoes are for running.*"). In addition, once premodified by intensifiers, the whole noun phrases will be ill-formed (e. g. * *the much dining room/* * *the quite running shoes*). Furthermore, they cannot take comparative or superlative forms (e. g. * *dininger/* * *diningest* or * *runninger/* * *runningest*). All these indicate that when gerunds premodify nouns, they manifest more nominal features than adjectival features. Consequently, similar to nominal modifiers, they look for the position closer to the HEAD noun than adjectives. This tendency explains the ungrammatical order cases of placing gerunds preceding adjectives, (e. g. * *dining new* and * *running hand-made*). More supports can be gained by the examples below.

(106) a. some sour green eating apples/ * some eating sour green apples

b. a huge electrical washing machine/ * a washing huge electrical machine

In accordance with some of semantic features of being a noun as has been described above, gerund forms "*eating*" in (106a) and "*washing*" in (106b) can naturally take the position closer to the HEAD nouns than do the other adjectives when they function as modifiers. And it would be unacceptable once adjectives are preceded by gerunds "*eating*" and "*washing*" in (106a) and (106b) to modify their HEAD nouns.

So far, the ordering of three types of modifiers has been examined depending on their respective semantic features. When a noun functions as a modifier, it continually remains many semantic features that a noun has, so to speak, they most of time occur in the prepositional object position; they are unable to be premodified by intensifiers, and they can never take the comparative or superlative forms as adjectives do. Thanks to the fact of sharing similar semantic features with its HEAD nouns, they take the position closest to the HEAD. When a gerund serves to be a modifier, it posits some features of being a noun: occurring in the position of prepositional object, unable to be premodified by intensifiers, unable to take the comparative or superlative forms. Consequently, they stay closer to the HEAD noun than adjectives. If an adjective acts as a modifier, it is able to be in the predicative position and can be premodified by intensifiers. If it co-exists with a noun or a gerund within a nominal phrase, it will definitely precede the noun or gerund modifiers. Referring to Haiman's conceptual distance, it can be stated as:

The more possible a prenominal modifier occurs in object position, the closer it is to the head noun;

The more possible a prenominal modifier is premodified by intensifiers, the less close it is to the head noun;

The more possible a prenominal modifier takes the comparative or superlative forms, the least close it is to the head noun.

Accordingly, the three types of modifiers are supposed to be ordered as follows:

(107) Ordering of adjectives, gerunds and nouns as prenominal modifiers within an NP

adjectives > gerunds or nouns > HEAD noun

Among the ordering principle rises a new question, that is, which has to be closer to the HEAD noun when a gerund together with a noun co-occurs within a noun phrase, since both of them bear at least three semantic features employed by a noun. The following examples are good cases in point.

(108) a. a <bamboo> fishing pole / * a fishing <bamboo> pole

b. <leather> riding boots / * riding <leather> boots

In examples (108a) and (108b), the nouns "*bamboo*", "leather" and gerunds "*fishing*", "*riding*" all exert the functions of being modifiers within the two noun phrases "*a bamboo fishing pole*" and "*leather riding boots*". However, they are acceptable merely when the noun modifier is preceded before the gerund modifier, while the reversed sequence is regarded as ungrammatical. Taking Haiman's conceptual distance principle into consideration, it could be implied that the conceptual intimacy between the element "*bamboo*" and the HEAD noun "*pole*" is less intensive than that between the element "*fishing*" and the HRAD "*pole*". Therefore they are placed in the order of "nouns > gerunds > HEAD noun". What can be the motivated mechanism behinds the type of linguistic phenomenon?

Kim (2007b) adds more plausibility to the conceptual closeness, who argues that the remote or intimate relation of a modifier with the HEAD frequently depends on human's perception and conceptual recognition of the entities on the world. When people mention the "*pole*" or the "*boots*", the primary question to be raised is possibly "what is that for?" or "what is the purpose or function of the thing?" rather than "what is made of (from)". Teyssier (1968) ever proposes that semantic functions of adjectivals can have impact on their ordering because when adjectivals serve to be modifiers, they inevitably constitute in a linear system a structure which demonstrates different relational degrees of signification among all the modifiers within a noun phrase. The modifier embodying the core function has the greatest intimacy thus will stay closest to the HEAD noun. This quite well provides the explanations to why gerund modifiers tend to take the position more intimate with the HEAD than noun modifiers. Whenever an entity is mentioned, people are inclined to be informed of its function or purpose earlier than its material. The linguistic correspondence to this conceptual representation naturally goes to the arrangement that the constituent designating semantic features of functions and use purposes of the entity is located closer to the center noun than the constituent denoting its materials. Accordingly, the ordering of the three types of modifiers, including adjectives, gerunds and nouns, can be rearranged into:

(109) The order of adjectives, gerunds and nouns as prenominal modifiers within a NOUN PHRASE: adjective > noun > gerund > HEAD NOUN

It is thus concluded that when modifiers have great distinctions among their semantic features, they can be ordered on accord of their semantic features. The elements that possess more semantic features of a noun, tend to stay closer to the HEAD, while the elements that have more semantic features holding by an adjective but less features owned by a noun, is left distant from the center noun. Given that modifiers share similar even the same semantic properties, the constituents conceptually designating the functions or use purposes of the entity will be placed intimate with head noun compared with those constituents that designate the materials. For more supports, take a look at the examples given below.

(110) a. antique < wood > writing desk/ * antique writing < wood > desk

b. an < iron > teaching rod/ * a teaching < iron > rod

5.4.2. The sequence of gerunds, adjectives and participles as prenominal modifiers

Certain modifiers in English are derived from verbs taking the past participle "-*ed*" form and the present participle "*-ing*" form. Although present participles are in form identical to gerunds, they are totally different syntactically and semantically. Traditional grammarians distinguish them by describing that present participles are fully adjectival and can usually be used with intensifiers, while gerunds cannot be premodified by intensifiers. Unclear and insufficient in both data and explanatory power, the distinction between them has always been a focus among linguistic researchers. Things are even more complicated when they go into a noun phrase to act as prenominal modifiers, as illustrated below.

(111) a. a sleeping boy

b. a sleeping car

(112) a. a soundly sleeping boy

b. * a soundly sleeping car

Native speakers can all at once notice the meaning differences of example (111a) from the example (111b) out of their intuitions. However, many of them are hard to identify, let alone explain, why an intensifier "*soundly*" can be grammatically added in front of the present participle "*sleeping*" in the example (112a), but not in front of the gerund "*sleeping*" as given in the example (112b), singly based on the rule listed by traditional grammarians.

In addition, similar to gerunds, the present participles usually do not occur alone as a prenominal modifier within a noun phrase. In our foregoing explanation, a gerund tend to be positioned closer to the HEAD noun when it appears within a noun phrase functioning as a prenominal modifier going together with other adjectives. What is the principle that should be observed by the present participle modifiers? Are the rules obeyed by gerund modifiers equally compatible with the present participle modifiers? More examples supplied below need to be considered:

(113) a. a <sleeping> little boy/ * a little <sleeping> boy

b. * a <sleeping> little car/a little <sleeping> car

It has been mentioned that if it has to be a modifier, a gerund occurs closer to the head noun than the adjective because semantically it possesses more semantic features of a noun than those bearing the semantic features of an adjective. This possibly can account for why the ordering of the noun phrase "*a little sleeping car*" in (113b) is well-formed, while ordering into the sequence "*a sleeping little car*" is unacceptable. The opposite goes to the example (113a), where the present participle modifier "*sleeping*" has to precede the adjective modifier "*little*" obtaining the initial position of the series of prenominal modifiers within the noun phrase. The question that immediately comes to mind can be what semantic features are mainly manifested to cause the present participles to be placed different from gerunds when both of them perform to be modifiers? The present study intends to refer to Quirk et al's explanation (1985) again to examine the semantic features of present participles when acting as modifiers. And it is hoped that the meaning explanation could be workable for the ordering motivation of present participles.

It has been verified that when functioning as modifiers, gerunds, if transformed into a simple clause, can never appear in the predicative position. Neither can they be premodified by intensifiers. That is to say, gerunds in effect demonstrate more meaning features of a noun rather than the meaning features of an adjective. Unlike gerunds, if transformed into a small clause, the present participle "*sleeping*" in example (113a) can grammatically take the predicative position (e. g. "*The boy is sleeping*"). In the meantime, the data in example (112a) implies that the present participle modifier "*sleeping*" can also be premodified by an intensifier, shown in the form "*the soundly sleeping boy*". Consequently, though identical in form, the present participle modifier "*sleeping*" has the semantic properties obviously distinctive from gerund modifier "*sleeping*" given in (113b). That can motivate humans to understand the reason why a present participle modifier is not allowed to be placed directly before the HEAD noun.

However, why should the present participle be placed more distant from the head than the adjective, as is given in the form "*a sleeping little boy*" in example (113a)? Syntactically speaking, a present participle is most of all derived from a verb form. In the process of transformation, it is deprived of the tense feature of a verb, with either the aspect or voice features remained. Despite of that, on account of the role of describing the happening of the action, the present participle is more or less imposed an "aspectual", or the "verbal" construal (Langacker 1991a, 1991b). Take the phrase (113a) for example, since the noun phrase "*a sleeping boy*" can be conceptually construed as "*a boy who is sleeping now*", the present participle "*sleeping*" here bears the aspectual feature of being progressive. It is this grammatical feature that keeps it distant from the center element of a noun phrase. The same account can be lent to the past participle, as shown in the phrase as follows:

(114) a. Indian running shoes/ * running Indian shoes

b. a neatly-dressed Indian woman/ * an Indian neatly-dressed woman

It is obviously seen in the example (114a), because the word "*running*" is a gerund, possessing the semantic properties of a noun, it occurs more intimate to the HEAD noun than its adjective modifier "*Indian*". Different from the gerund modifier "*running*", the word form "*neatly-dressed*" in (114b) has the semantic properties of being an adjective for the reason that it can occur in the predicative position and can be premodified by an intensifier, (e. g. the grammatical phrase "*so neatly-dressed Indian woman*"). In the meantime, it remains its perfective property that a verb form usually posits. Therefore, it is actually not completely transformed into an adjective. The word class of it goes between an adjective and a verb. It could be easy to understand past participle modifier goes further than the adjective modifier "*Indian*" within the noun phrase "*a neatly-dressed Indian woman*". Any reverse is proved to be impossible. These semantic explanations for past participles appear to gain more supports from the examples that follow.

(115) a. a nobly born young man

b. a lightly built eight-stone person

An analogous explanation can be given to the examples in (115). Both the past participle modifier "*nobly born*" in example (115a) and the modifier form "*lightly built*" in example (115b) take initial position, going before the adjectives "*young*" and "*eight-stone*" for the reason that though they take the semantic features and syntactic position of an adjective, they remain in small portion their verbal features, so to speak, perfective property. Therefore, they are alien from both adjectives and gerunds and consequently, they are located remote to the HEAD noun.

In an effort to account for the semantic features of gerunds, present participles and past participles when they appear a nominal phrase functioning to be modifiers, it is concluded that a gerund modifier occurs closer to the HEAD noun because of its possession of semantic properties of a noun. On the contrary, present or past participles precede both the adjective and gerund modifiers in that they proportionally remain their aspectual properties inherent by a verb and thus cannot be seen identical to the prenominal adjectives. Linked again to the distance principle of iconicity by Haiman (1985), the explanation to the prenominal modifier ordering among (present or past) participles and adjectives can be generalized as in rule (116).

(116) a. The more adjective properties a prenominal modifier possesses, the closer it is to the HEAD noun.

b. The more verbal properties a prenominal modifier possesses, the remoter it is to the HEAD noun.

Based on this generalization, the ordering principle of pronominal modifiers including the gerunds, (present or past) participles, adjectives and nouns can be integrated and reorganized into:

(117) Linear order of gerunds, adjectives, nouns and participles as prenominal modifiers

(Past or present) participles > adjectives > nouns > gerunds > HEAD

5.4.3. The placement of denominal adjectives as prenominal modifiers

Adjectives with such suffixes as *-ic(al)*, *-i(al)*, *-en*, *-ary*, etc. are defined as denominal adjectives, because they are derivatives of nouns. Quirk et al (1972: 922) observed and summarized that the denominal adjectives, containing the meaning "consisting of", "involving", or "relating to" can be prepositioned before a wide range of premodifying items and they can even come directly next before the head, as shown in example (118) below.

(118) a. historical novels

b. photographical equipment

This group of adjectives stays close to the center noun for the reason that they are derived from nouns in nature and characteristic of to certain degree being nominal in nature. They endow the head nouns with the attributes of the nouns, from which they are derived. It is also found by Quirk et al (1985) that denominal adjectives can syntactically be converted into prepositional phrase forms within a clause. That is to say, the noun phrase "*historical novels*" is changed into the noun phrase "*novels about history*" with its modifier postponed. Correspondingly, the noun phrase "*photographical equipment*" is rephrased into the form "*equipment for making photographs*".

Denominal adjectives are so unique in semantic properties and syntactic placing that people are curious that if the denominal adjectives have to co-exist with other pronominal modifiers within a noun phrase, what will be their ordering principles? Necessarily, observation of the relevant data is the way to dig out the solution of the problem.

(119) a. a *political* problem

Denominal + HEAD

b. *badly copied Gothic church* tower

P. P. + Denominal + noun + HEAD

c. *delicate*, *intricate traditional* design

Adjective + Denominal + HEAD

d. the *newly-designed industrial washing* machine

P. P. + Denominal + gerund + HEAD

It is observed in examples (119) together with a body of data collection, when acting as modifiers, a denominal adjective usually occurs before a noun modifier, as shown in (119b) (i. e. *Gothic* precedes *church.*). Opposite to the example (119b), the phrase in (119c) indicates that denominal adjectives have to follow the past participle (shortened into P. P.) and also adjective as given in (119c). When a (present or past) participle, a gerund and a denominal adjective co-exist to modify the head noun within a noun phrase, the denominal adjective is inclined to stay in between the participle modifier and the gerund modifier as shown in (119d). When separating denominal adjective from adjective and including it independently into the prenominal modifier ordering classification, the result is shown in principle (120). Even though bearing an adjective form, because they are derivatives of nouns and inherited many nominal features from its original noun forms, denominal adjectives take the position between adjective and gerund modifiers.

(120) The ordering principle of (present or past) particples, adjectives, denominal adjectives, nouns and gerunds as prenominal modifiers:

(present or past) Participle > Adjective > Denominal adjective > Noun > Gerund > HEAD

To sum up this section, it is investigated that among the prenominal modifier forms including (present or past) particples, adjectives, denominal adjectives, nouns and gerunds, the closer the prenominal modifier is to the HEAD noun, the more nominal properties it has. Supporting evidence for this claim comes from this fact: when nouns and gerunds serve as the modifiers, they stay closest to the head noun. Relying on Haiman's conceptual closeness, linguistic closeness reflects conceptual closeness which in turn implies the similar semantic properties between them. Our detailed examination further proves that linguistic distance between the HEAD and its modifiers reflects their semantic distance. The statement can be summarized into what is called in this study "The Principle of Nouniness". ①

(121) The Principle of Nouniness for Prenominal Modifiers:

---

① The reason I use "nouniness" instead of "nominal" is that the semantic properties of prenominal modifiers are in a level of gradient degree, which is not discrete in categories. The term "nouniness" was first utilized by Ross (1973) to describe the different extents to which a particular constituent functions like a noun.

a. The more nominal properties a prenominal modifier has, the closer to the head noun.

b. The more adjective properties a prenominal modifier has, the less close to the head noun.

c. The more verbal properties a prenominal modifier has, the least close to the head noun.

In terms of the Principle of Nouniness for Prenominal Modifers given out above in (121), the general order of prenominal modifier can be reestablished as follows:

(122) The general order principle of prenominal modifiers among an NP:

(Past and Present) Participles > Adjectives > Denominal Adjectives > Nouns > Gerunds > HEAD NOUN

5.5. Gradability degree of prenominal adjectives

Owing to the fact that most of the prenominal modifiers in English are constituted by adjectives, the motivation of sequencing prenominal adjectives in different orders need to be looked into. Adjectives describe qualities or characteristics of nouns. Most of the qualities are varied in intensity or "grade". Thus the explanation of the sequence of English prenominal adjectives needs to conduct an intensive study of the characteristics of "gradability" in English adjectives.

5.5.1. Traditional classifications of adjectives

Lehrer (1985) claims his "Semantic Fields" theory to prove the gradable/ungradable polarity of adjectives. He proposes that adjectives be divided into two semantic fields: descriptors and classifiers. The former describe the quality of people or things (e.g. *big*, *small*, *tall*, *far*, *beautiful*, *graceful*, *hot*, *dirty*, etc.); the latter indicate the categories to which people or things belong (e. g. *plastic*, *Chinese*, *medical*, *geographic*, *scientific*, *dead*, etc.)

Similarly, in the two famous grammar books, *A Comprehensive Grammar of the English Language* complied by Quirk et al (1985) and *A New English Grammar* by Zhang (1997) in China, English adjectives are classified into two complementary polarities: gradable and ungradable adjectives. The gradable adjectives are featured in the ability of describing the qualities of nouns that can vary in intensity or "grade" and the ability of being modified by intensifiers, such as "*very*", "*extremely*", "*a little*", while the ungradable ones on the contrary cannot describe the nouns with qualities of various intensity or grade, neither can they be modified by intensifiers. It is quite clear that gradable adjectives correspond to descriptors, and ungradable adjectives are to classifiers.

The reason that gradable adjectives can be modified by intensifiers is attributed to a strong subjective orientation by a handful of researchers. They explain that judging the quality of an object needs any individual to possess a criterion inherent in his/her mind. The criteria for gradable adjectives are usually based on people's experiences and vary from different situations or from different entities to be modified. Take a look into the gradable adjective "*tall*" in the following examples:

(123) a. a tall man

b. a tall building

It is seen that the same gradable adjective "*tall*" is used in both the phrase (123a) and the phrase (123b) to denote the height of the concrete entities "*man*" and "*building*". However, when listeners decode the meanings of the two phrases, the criteria for judging the height of a person and a building will be totally different: a six-inch man can possibly be "*a tall man*", while *a* six-inch building cannot even be considered a building at all. It therefore shows that although a single adjective "*tall*" is applicable in both phrases, the semantic properties are understood distinctively according to the different features signified by different nouns with which the adjective is modifying.

Compared to gradable adjectives, ungradable adjectives are less complex to identify, and they are often used alone or with "non-grading adverbs". As given in the examples (124a)-(124e):

(124) a. It was φ *freezing* outside.

b. The dog was φ *dead*.

c. Her exam results were *absolutely awful*. She will have to take the exam again.

d. Is there anything like it in the world? It must be *virtually unique*.

e. It starts an *essentially chemical* reaction.

Thanks to the attributes, the ungradable adjectives can be further divided into five sub-fields by Lehrer (1985), according to the semantic distinctions listed below:

(125) a. Material: electric, metallic, plastic, golden, silken, wooden, woolly, etc.

b. Origin: English, Chinese, American, French, etc.

c. Subject and discipline: academic, agricultural, chemical, atomic, commercial, cultural, economical, historical, etc.

d. Geometric shape: oval, oblong, cubic, triangle, round, square, parallel, horizontal, etc.

e. Complementary contrast: alive, dead, male, female, married, single, true, false, present, absent, etc.

The traditional notion of gradable and ungradable adjectives seems to provide a clear and acceptable classification in dealing with adjectives, and also highlights the characteristics of gradable adjectives because they bear basic attributes of adjectives. Based on prototype theory (Taylor 2001), gradable adjectives reside in the prototypical members of adjectives, while ungradable ones fall into the non-prototypical category. Lakoff and Johnson (1987: 21) equally hold that some categories do not have gradation of membership, while others do. A good case in point is a category like *gender* (*male or female*). One can only have two complementary choices: to be male or to be female. On the contrary, the adjectives "rich" and "tall" in the nominal phrases like "*rich people*" or "*a tall man*" are able to be graded, simply because there are gradations of richness and tallness in human cognitive process.

As far as their placements within a noun phrase are concerned, many experts fail to make a satisfactory conclusion. However, many studies, through intensive observations into the data and introspective reflections from native speakers, clearly state the fact that ungradable adjectives are always positioned closer to the head noun than gradable adjectives within a single nominal phrase when both of them have to appear simultaneously to modify a central noun, as is shown in (126) below.

(126) a. an <old> French golden watch

b. those <boring> commercial advertisements

In the example (126) that the gradable adjectives "*old*" and "*boring*" co-occur with ungradable adjectives "*French*", "*golden*" and "*commercial*" because the three words respectively identify the origin, the material and the discipline of the head nouns "*watch*" and "*advertisement*". When entering into a single phrase, it is obvious that gradable adjectives as "*old*" in (126a) and "*boring*" in (126b) take the positions further from the head than ungradable ones (i. e. "*golden*" in (126a) and "*commercial*" in (126b)). The question that arises right now will be what is the motivation behind sequencing the adjectives into logical order when gradable and ungradable adjectives exist together in a single noun phrase? The problem will get more blurred if two or more gradable or ungradable adjectives occur simultaneously within a noun phrase, what will be the decisive principle to arrange the elements into right sequence? Or seeing two ungradable adjectives come out together with a noun phrase, is it easy for human to recognize that there is actually no abrupt transition from one polarity to the other?

(127) The moon in Tokyo is rounder than in Beijing.

No native speakers will question the grammaticality of the sentence in (127). However, it is quite natural for people to ask since all people on the earth have a shared moon, what are the maxims used by the speakers who judge, believe and utter that the moon in Tokyo is rounder than the moon in Beijing. It will be a good guess that the speaker is from Japan and out of the sense of nationality glory, he or she tends to make such a subjective judgement perhaps. Reversely suppose that the speaker were a Chinese, the sentence would possibly be "The moon in Beijing is rounder than in Tokyo". What confused us is which on earth is rounder, the moon in Japan or the moon in China? It in the meantime goes against our common sense that all human have a shared moon and it will be seen the same. What is revealed here is that within the group of adjectives and even within a single gradable adjectives, their gradation is not on the same level. Then a question arises on how to make a scientific classification of those adjectives to specify their ordering before the head noun?

In order to model graded categories, Zadeh (1965) devises a fuzzy set theory, distinguished from the classical set theory, which says that all the things in the world have a clear boundary which helps classify things either in the set (having membership value 1) or outside the set (having membership value 0). In addition to that, Zadeh proves in his Fuzzy Set Theory, more values can be allowed between value 0 and value 1. Many examples can be easily found where adjectives are used in sentences with a fuzzy comparative degree. This corresponds to Zadeh's intuition that concerning about their heights, some persons are neither absolutely tall nor absolutely short, but in the middle-tall to certain extent. In the original version of fuzzy set theory, operations on fuzzy sets are simple generalizations of operations on ordinary sets:

(128) Suppose element x has membership value in fuzzy set A and membership value w in fuzzy set B.

Intersection: the value of x in $A \cap B$ is the minimum of v and w.

Union: the value of x in $A \cup B$ is the calibration of v and w.

Complement: the value of x in the complement of A is $1-v$.

(Zadeh, 1965)

This is a natural and ingenious elaboration of the classical theory of sets. Unfortunately, many scholars think it to be too mathematic and too sophisticated when they are applied into the field of language studies, in particular the research of the fuzzy degrees of adjectives because the understanding of adjectives can never stay without the understanding of the inherent lexical meanings. Despite of these, this study embraces the literature contributions to further propose a notion of "gradability degree principle" to make a classification among adjectives no matter they are gradable or ungradable. The process of classifying is given as follows: different adjectives (either gradable or ungradable adjectives) are first subjected to some general properties of adjectives, and gradability degree is judged by how many properties each adjective has. The intention is to make a clearer distinction among the adjectives by means of quantitative study of various adjective features. It is hoped that the distinction of adjectives under the gradability degree principle will be helpful for language users to arrange the order of adjectives within a noun phrase.

5.5.2. Principles of Gradability Degree

Six calibrations are selected to constitute a scale of gradability, so to speak, subjectivity, relativity, cultural variation, continuity, immeasurability and non-prototype. The first three calibrations are characteristic of the typical gradable adjectives because they have already internalized by human beings when people perceive the things in the world. They are a combination of the characteristics of the perceiver and the perceived entities in the cognitive process. Through the conceptualization towards their perceptions, the objective and physical concepts are reflected in the human brain.

The calibration of continuity comes from the most prominent quantitative features of gradable or ungradable adjectives for the reason that they can be premodified by the intensifiers (e. g. *The children are very happy.*); they can take comparative and superlative forms inflectionally (e. g. *The children are happier now.*) (Guirk *et all* 1972:231 – 232). All the other five calibrations will be detailedly elaborated in below.

Subjectivity

Entities, no matter they objectively exist or not, will be conceptualized and finally reflected in human mind with the print of personal experiences. It is at this level of physical experience and on this ground of conceptualization process that human beings can accurately distinguish tigers from elephants, chairs from tables, roses from daffodils, asparagus from broccoli, copper from lead, etc. (Lakoff and Johnson 1987: 269).

Despite of the fact that physical experiences play a crucial role in the cognitive process, they are inevitably of individual variations. The cause can be explained in the way that individuals are separately brought up under a particular environment, which amounts to the differences in their social and educational backgrounds, religious and political beliefs, economic conditions and ways of living. These factors, along with personal physical traits like sex and age, constitute the extraordinary life experiences of an individual. Variation in personal experiences leads to variation in the cognitive mode. Therefore, the concepts of the entity accordingly vary from person to person, no matter how many they have in common in both quality and quantity. As the proverb goes,

"One man's meat is another man's poison." It implies that the subjectivity and its degree do exist in human minds. Different from nouns and verbs that are respectively used to represent the entities in the physical world and the process of the entities that take place in the world, adjectives designate the attributes of physical things and need more cognitive process of human beings that are inclined to be subjective to certain degree. The implied comprehension of subjectivity reflects an internalized scale that a person would intuitively draw on in forming a concept about the objective existence. These scales, originated from personal experiences, are of the obvious subjectivity of comprehension: different individuals would cause various evaluations on a single entity or affair due to their subjectivity of comprehension.

Relativity

It refers to the feature that when used to modify a head noun, the characteristics revealed by the adjectives are usually dependent on the specific attributes of the head nouns. Take the sentence "*Not many people were present*" for example. The exact number of people never changelessly remains the same. Instead, depending on the variety of locations, it might be five or six if a birthday party is referred to, or as many as twenty thousand in the case of an international Cognitive Linguistics Conference.

The significance of relativity exists in the collocation of gradable adjectives with various kinds of head nouns. The semantic strength of gradable adjectives is determined by the relative semantic features possessed in the noun phrases, and is therefore a variation on the semantic level. Furthermore, when the head noun refers to an extra-linguistic entity, the semantic strength of the head restricts the perception of the modifier. Take for instance the adjectives "*tall*" and "*long*" in the following phrases.

(129) a. a tall man

b. a tall tree

(130) a. long river

b. long hair

c. long finger

The height of the word "man" will be conceptualized differently from the height of the word "tree" in the two phrases of example (129), because the viewers will take two different reference objects to cognize the concept of the two linguistic forms. Example (129a) takes the average height of men as its referent, while the average height indicated in example (129b) takes the height of generic trees as referent. Under this preconditioned standards that average height of the man in the physical world might not reach the average height of the tree, the two phrases can be decoded that there is a discrepancy between the height of the man and the height of the tree and the actual height of a tree is probably taller than that of a man. Even the tallest man in the world cannot reach the average height of trees. The same account goes to the three noun phrases in example (130). Due to the different domain of their reference objects, their actual lengths of different subjects like "river", "hair" and "finger" vary significantly.

Wang (2001: 174) claims that when gradable adjectives collocate with different nominal nouns, the meanings of adjectives are made less vague by supplying the following examples referring to the adjective "old".

(131) old cake	several hours, several days or several months
old car	eight to ten years
old dog	above ten years
old man	above sixty or eighty years
old star	above zillions of years

It is apparent that the actual age that the gradable adjective "*old*" denotes is actually determined by the specific nominal it collocates with. Though dogs, men and stars can live only within a limited period of time, their life expectancies are of great diversity. A ten-year-old dog will be seen old because their average life expectancy is ten to twenty years. A man can live approximately for seventy to ninety years under normal circumstances and the common sense tells that a man above sixty should be respected for being an elderly man. As far as stars in the space are concerned, a star of several billions years old is technically considered a young one. Therefore, the exact meaning of a single linguistic form "*old*", if employed to modify different entities, can extend from a few hours to zillions of years, or even the infinite.

Cultural Variation

The cultural mode determines people's comprehension of language. Earlier researches from Chomsky have found that when rich in cultural connotation, language, as the carrier of a certain culture, conveys boundless cultural information. It implies that the comprehension of a language phenomenon is heavily reliable on the cultural environment shared by the speech community. Ungerer and Schmid (1996) state from the perspective of Cognitive Linguistics that the reason that the prototypes for a category are not absolutely invariable, but relatively stable is they would vary with the change of context and environments. Therefore, the variations of prototypes are dependent on the cognitive models internalized in human mind, and in turn an individual's cognitive models are ultimately determined by the cultural models which he or she is involved in. Cruse (1990: 389) points out that the prototype of a category is obviously influenced by the degree of familiarity and the conceptualization process through the personal experiences of the world from the subject. Geographical condition, historical heritage, economic and political condition of the speech community can all be regarded as factors deciding people's comprehension of a linguistic form. The well-known poem written by Shelley "Ode to the West Wind" is a good case. Different from the persons who live in the southern hemisphere and consider the west wind as the arrival of spring based on their embodiment of the four seasons, the people inhabitant in the northern hemisphere, would consider the west wind as the connotation of the coming of autumn.

In the meantime, the evaluative standard of the poverty states in the developed countries is definitely different from that of poverty states in less developed countries. Take the two sentences given in example (132) for instance:

(132) a. He is *poor* and lives in an apartment with *little* furniture.

b. He is *rich* and lives in an apartment with *good* furniture.

In describing the economic condition of a person, people from developed countries may use sentence (132a), while people from undeveloped countries would most likely use sentence (132b).

It is widely acknowledged that distinctions in cognition do exist among individuals and among cross-cultural interactions, and many misunderstandings from cultural variations may more or less hinder the facilitation of communication. However under normal circumstances where the variation is comparatively minor and subtle, communicative gaps may be bridged through context and non-verbal assistances.

Immeasurability

Immeasurability means that the quality that an adjective depicts cannot be measured by a clear scientific calibration, either physical or chemical. The term *scientific calibration* is used to refer to a calibration which can scientifically measure or define the quality of the adjective. The adjectives that can be measured by the scientific calibration are apt to ungradability and those that cannot are inclined to gradability. For example, the adjective "*big*" is used to describe the size of entities and can be measured by square measures or cubical measures and the adjectives like "*wooden*" and "*plastic*" can be measured by their special molecular structures. Therefore, these adjectives are measurable. The gradable adjective "*beautiful*" is opposite because one can hardly find an objective scale to measure it.

Non-prototype

Prototype in Cognitive Linguistics refers to the best example of a category. Although a category can be universal, few universal prototypes exist. Despite of that, universal prototype is still considered as a prototype accepted by human beings from a variety of encyclopedia backgrounds. Some universal prototypes are context independent, and have the attributes described to be ungradable adjectives such as "*iron*, *metal*, *wooden* and *plastic*, *etc*". Oppositely, non-prototype means that there is no universally best prototype for the quality that an adjective describes. For example, the adjective "*tall*" is non-prototype because there is no identical scale deciding the definite height of the two noun phrases "*a tall building*" and "*a tall man*".

5.5.3. Illustrations

To help understand the six calibrations of judging adjective degrees, a good illustration is quite necessary. To fulfill that, five commonly-used adjectives representing respectively five different semantic features are finally chosen as examples in the study. Their adjectival characteristics will be illustrated based on the six calibrations, and consequently, the reasons for their acquisition of or deficiency in the values of the adjectives will be provided. Accordingly, the relation between the gradability degree and the position of the adjectives within a noun phrase will be also hypothesized. It is assumed that the more properties an adjective has, the higher its gradability degree is, and the further it takes the position from the head noun.

The adjectives chosen for discussion are the most prototypical of the kind: *beautiful*, *big*, *round*, *red* and *plastic*. The adjective "*beautiful*" represents the kind of adjectives that give the general description entities denoted by nouns and have a strong inclination of subjectivity. The other examples this group are "*brave*, *courageous*, *poor*, *charming*, *dirty*", and so on. The adjective "*big*" represents those which make subjective judgment of the sizes of objects, e. g. "*small*, *long*, *short*, *high*, *tall*", and the like. The adjective "*round*" represents the group of adjectives denoting the shapes of objects, e. g. "*triangular*, *oblong*, *oval*", etc. The adjective "*red*" is the representative of the color terms. The last adjective chosen "*plastic*" stands for those ungradable adjectives which depict the material of physical entities.

5. 5. 3. 1. "Beautiful"

The adjective "*beautiful*", as a typical gradable adjective, has a strong inclination of subjectivity, relativity and cultural variation. A very explicit example exists in the evaluation of movie stars from subjective attitudes. A lot of people will consider a female movie star very attractive while in other people's eyes, she is very rustic. As for relativity, which mainly refers to the different meaning inferred from the collocation with different nouns, the scale for judging the beauty of people cannot be used to judge that of animals although there may exist something in common. The adjective "beautiful" is a quite typical example of cultural variations. In some primitive tribes, women with tattoos on their faces are considered beautiful. In some African tribes, women who have long necks are considered beautiful and will be worshiped by males in their tribes.

The best way to test the value of continuity is using intensifier adverbs such as "*very*, *a little*, *extremely*". If the adjective can be modified by them, the adjective embodies the value of continuity. "*Beautiful*" is one of the examples because adjective phrases like "*very beautiful*" and "*extremely beautiful*" are frequently heard in English. Owing to the complexity and subjectivity of the quality in the adjective "*beautiful*", no calibration is applied for scientific measurements of it. Therefore, it is immeasurable. Maybe some people will say that the popular notion of vital statistics (i. e. chest, waist and bottom measurement of a woman), which is prevailing in the world of fashion, can be used as the criterion of judgment. However, this notion is far from unanimity and generality. We cannot find a typical prototype of beautiful woman which satisfies all in diverse cultures.

If the presence of each calibration is scaled with number "1", the absence of the calibration with number "0", the total of the adjective "beautiful" can amount to 6.

5.5.3.2. "Big"

The second chosen adjective "*big*" is also a typical gradable adjective with the presence of the first three values of being gradable adjectives. Look at the phrase "*a big ball*". The earth is a big ball in the eyes of ordinary people; however, as to an astronomer, it is only a small heavenly body in the indefinite universe. To most average Chinese citizens in a city, an apartment of 100 square meters is big enough, whereas it is not that spacious for a rich businessman, who has a villa of three stores. This proves the value of subjectivity. In terms of the value of relativity, the size of "*a big orange*" is undoubtedly smaller than the size of a big man or a big house. Of course, the adjective "*big*" has also acquired the value of cultural variation. "*A big man*" in Japan is smaller than "*a big man*" in white people's eyes because the genetic heritage of the two races is different, and the ordinary size of white people is bigger than that of Asian people. Besides, it is quite safe to modify the adjective "*big*" with the intensifiers "*very*, *a little* and *extremely*" etc. Therefore, the word "*big*" owns the value of continuity.

Besides that the linguistic form "*big*" has the four values of gradable adjectives, it has the characteristics of measurability which most ungradable adjectives have, because the adjective "*big*" is used to describe the shape of an entity, which is based on the physical calibration of size measured by the square, being a two-dimensional calibration, or the cube, being a three-dimensional calibration. It is hard to find a universal prototype for "*a big ball*" because of the quality of subjectivity and relativity. Thus the values of the adjective "big" go straight next to the adjective "beautiful", totaling 5.

5.5.3.3. "Round"

The adjective "*round*" represents a special type of adjectives whose qualities make it stay between the gradable and the ungradable adjectives. Owing to the specificity of the adjective "*round*", our discussion begins with the last two values which are often deficient in ungradable adjectives.

The word "*round*" is measurable, because it can be measured by a scientific calibration of a geometric scale defined with the same length from every point in the outline to the center. According to the notion proposed by Gestalt psychology, circles, squares and equilateral triangles are assumed to be perceptually salient among geometrical shapes (Ungerer and Schmid 1996: 10). A typical round entity (both two-dimensional and three-dimensional) whose outline is circular (not oval or triangular) is considered a prototype of the category it belongs to.

Although "*round*" is deficient in the last two values which typical gradable adjectives convey, it is not without the other values. The value of subjectivity shows that roundedness is perceived differently by different individuals. There exist different degrees of roundedness between a perfect round entity and an oval. When people look at objects such as the moon in the sky, cakes or oranges, they just apply their experience to the description of the shapes instead of using a pair of compasses to measure whether the objects are perfectly round or approximately round. Admittedly, objects like the moon or drops of morning dew on leaves cannot be measured precisely by average people. But the value of subjectivity is quite limited in this item. Because of the existence of a prototype, *round* in any degree should conform to the prototype. If you regard an oval as round, you deviate a little far from the calibration. In some circumstances, it is acceptable. An oval rugby ball, for instance, is not literally a ball but is referred to as a football in American English. However, nobody would accept it if a triangle shape, a pyramid for example, was described as round, which is too far away from the calibration.

When the adjective "*round*" is used to describe the form or appearance of entities, people choose it as the implied reference object. Whatever it is, from a round face, a round melon, a round cake to a round moon, the referent is the unique— being round. Thus the comprehension scope elicited by the collocation with different entities is almost the same. In this sense, it is safe to say that the feature of relativity does not apply to this adjective. As there is a scientific calibration which is completely objective in the concept of being round and because the implied reference object when people perceive the concept "*round*", we can believe that the universal culture supposedly plays its role here. Thus there is no cultural variation in perceiving the word and its collocation with different nouns. Moreover, the adjective "*round*" can be modified by the intensifiers such as "*very*, *rather*", or "*extremely*". Therefore, it embodies the value of continuity.

5.5.3.4. "Red"

The commonly-mentioned adjective "*red*" belongs to the color terms that is quite special in that they not only reflect qualities of the extra-linguistic entity but the cognition of them is the process of the cooperation of the visual nerve system and the human cognitive ability.

Earlier research shows that Dugun Dani, a language spoken by Dani, contains only two basic color terms, in contrast to the eleven basic color terms available to speakers of English (Heider 1970, Ungerer and Schmid 1996: 6). This difference in vocabulary results from the different comprehension of colors by the two groups of peoples. Likewise, as a result of their special life experience, the Eskimos have a larger and richer vocabulary of snow than English-speaking people do. Kay and McDaniel (1978) explain the process people perceive focal colors in the theory of fuzzy boundary: the cognition of colors by people is the product under the functioning of the visual nervous system and the human cognitive ability. It is not absolutely objective and independent from the perceiver but is engendered from the combination of the real world, people's physiological function and cognitive mechanism which is regarded as fuzzy boundary and cultural selection. They point out that people's physiological characteristics influence the forming of color notions and language expression (Zhao 2001: 42) so it can be concluded that color terms are endowed with the values of subjectivity and cultural variation.

With the help of the color card, Berlin and Kay (1969) set about testing how speakers of the twenty selected languages categorize colors. The experiment shows that focal colors are not only shared by the speakers of one and the same language but they are also very consistent across different languages. There is compelling evidence that instead of being arbitrary, color categorization is anchored in focal colors. While the boundaries of color categories vary among languages and even among speakers of the same language, focal colors are shared by different speakers and even different language communities. Focal colors can be the best examples of colors, which appear to possess a particular perceptual-cognitive salience, which is probably independent of language. In view of research by Kay and McDaniel (1978) we might even say that the salience of focal colors reflects certain physiological aspects of man's perceptive mechanisms. Another line of explanation relates focal colors to certain universally occurring phenomena like day and night (white and black), the sun (red), vegetation (green), the sky (blue) and the ground (brown) (Wierzbicka 1990b). Instead of the term "focal colors" used by Berlin and Kay (1969), Rosch (1978) employs "natural prototype", which is the most salient example of the category and is perceived with the least effort. Therefore color terms have the value of prototype and acquire zero point in the value of non-prototype.

Owing to the fact that colors are constituted by means of hue, brightness and saturation, which make them capable of being recognized and classified, the calibration of immeasurability is challenged. The three scales contribute to making subtle and scientific classification of colors. It is not difficult to give a color a scientific name if we examine its hue, brightness and saturation. According to the three scales, people make colors which are often used by students in fine arts to recognize colors. Therefore, the value of immeasurability is absent in color terms.

As the boundary of a color is quite vague, (the fuzzy boundary between red and orange for instance), continuity is the nature of color terms. Centering on a focal color, the three elements cause colors to change according to certain rules, thus resulting in a clusters of colors. To put it more explicitly, we have red in the center, darker colors like scarlet, crimson, purple, etc, at one end, and lighter colors like orange, pink, etc, at the other end. There are no clear boundaries between these colors. In this sense, we can believe that color terms acquire the value of continuity.

However, it is a tough task to illustrate the relativity value of color terms. Relativity lies in the collocation. In collocations like "*red apple*", "*red face*", or "*red co*at", their reference object is the same— the focal color "red". Different nominal hosts may lead to slight difference in comprehension of the color, but the implied measurement of these colors always conform to the domain of the focal color. Therefore, the adjective "*red*" is deficient in the value of relativity.

5.5.3.5. "Plastic"

Denoting to the specific molecular structure of the entities, the quality of the word "*plastic*", similar to material quality modifiers like "*metal*", "*wooden*", or "*glass*", can be referred to as the physical, chemical calibration of the material and provide scientific calibration for measurement. Therefore, the adjective "*plastic*" is deficient in the value of immeasurability. It is very easy to find the prototypical example of a plastic entity because any material whose molecular structure is in accordance with the plastic molecular structure can be its best example. Accordingly, the adjective "*plastic*" has the salient characteristics of ungradable adjectives and lacks the four positive values of gradable adjectives.

All in all, the calibration standards including subjectivity, relativity, cultural variation, immeasurability and non-prototype, evaluate adjectives from cognitive perspectives. The first two are inclined to highlight the characteristics of cognitive activities from the variation perspectives of individuals and of language communities. The last two are the cognitive activities from cognitive performers concerning the characteristics of the bodily-experienced entities in the world. The calibration of relativity evaluates adjectives from semantic perspective, examining meanings of adjectives resulting from the collocation with different head nouns. The calibration of continuity examines the quantitative features of adjectives from the cognitive semantic angle.

The purpose of putting forward the notion of gradability degrees of adjectives is to prove that the degrees of gradability of adjectives are related to the ordering of prenominal adjectives in English. Therefore, a diagram is employed to show the values each adjective contains depending on the six calibrations. The total value is a reflection of the gradability degree of each selected adjective. The specific illustrations are given in Table 4. The figures in Table 4 have shown the total value of gradability that each adjective has given is an easy and clear way of protruding the differences and relations of the five selected adjectives.

Table 4: Gradability Degrees of Five Representative Adjectives

	Subjectivity	Relativity	Cultural variation	Continuity	Immea-surability	Non-prototype	Total value
Beautiful	1	1	1	1	1	1	6
Big	1	1	1	1	0	1	5
Round	1	0	0	1	0	0	2
Red	1	0	1	1	0	0	3
Plastic	0	0	0	0	0	0	0

Thanks to the six calibrations of scaling the gradability degrees of adjectives in English as is shown in Table 4, the differences and relations among these adjectives are strongly protruded. The question proposed next is obviously what the degrees of gradability of adjectives can contribute to the arrangement of the prenominal adjective ordering in English? After a large quantity of selected data are observed and then analyzed, the concluding remarks are finally made.

The present study read through many up-to-date English magazines and journals and collected enough nominal phrases with more than two adjectives as their premodifiers included. Every single adjective within the phrase has been closely analyzed on the ground of six calibrations to judge their gradability degrees. They are listed and illustrated as follows:

(133) a. a very useful small oblong tin box

b. a beautiful exclusive large black resident district

c. ridiculous little green metal tables

In example (133a), based on the six values used to judge the gradability of the adjectives, the adjective "*useful*" possesses the highest on the scale of the gradability level (i. e. value 6); the adjective "*small*" bearing five values, comes to the second (i. e. value 5); the adjective "*oblong*" which is referring to the shape comes next because it totals the value of 2; the last adjective "*tin*" is the lowest level in the example (133a). The same analysis can solve the problem in examples (133b) and (133c): the adjectival modifiers "*exclusive*" and "*ridiculous*" should precede those referring to shapes and colors, and those of materials like the ones "*metal*" having the lowest gradability level come to the last in the sequence. The whole phrase should be ordered like this:

(134) a. very useful (6) small (5) oblong (2) tin (0) box

b. a beautiful (6) exclusive (6) large (5) black (3) resident (0) district

c. ridiculous (6) little (5) green (3) metal (0) tables

More examples are supplied with in their gradability level as below.

(135) a. a good (6) small (5) round (2) table

b. a distinguished (6) American (0) literary (0) man

c. these beautiful (6) tiny (5) round (2) crystals

d. a long (5) white (3) Chinese (0) gown

e. an excellent (6) white (3) sports (0) car

f. some sour (6) green (3) eating (0) apples

A more typical example is provided with detailed description to persuade into the validity and credibility of gradability degrees :

(136) some beautiful large round red plastic chairs

In the example (136), the modifier "*beautiful*" has the highest gradability level (i. e. value 6), the adjective "*large*" goes to the second (i. e. value 5), and the adjective "*plastic*" has the lowest gradability level (i. e. value 0). The phrase has been sequenced in the order given below:

(137) some beautiful (6) large (5) *round* (2) *red* (3) plastic (0) chairs

In this example, an obvious inconsistency is found between the gradability level and the sequence of the adjectives referring to the shape and color. Disagreement arises when adjectives concerning color terms are juxtaposed with adjectives referring to shapes. Because of the complexity of the nature of color terms, it is difficult for people to make an objective evaluation of the values of their gradability. According to the idiomatic usage, color terms often follow adjectives referring to shapes, for example in the nominal phrases "*a pretty small round pink face*", "*a round brown wooden table*", "*a triangular yellow card*" and "*an oblong dark ground*". Only in some marked cases do color terms precede adjectives indicating shapes, as in a phrase like "*a red oblong wooden box*", where the adjective "*oblong*" is stressed by exchanging the placement with the adjective "red". However, as an unmarked form like "*an oblong red wooden box*" is an ordinary description of the entity without any pragmatic connotation.

Through the observation of the large body of the data concerned with the English nominal phrases, what can be generalized about the relation between the gradability degrees and the position of the adjectives within a noun phrase, if related to the distance principle, again would be like the following statement:

(138) Judged from the six calibrations on the gradability degree

a. the lower a prenominal adjective is in the gradability degrees, the closer to the head noun

b. the higher a prenominal adjective in the gradability degrees, the more distant to the head noun.

5. 6. Discussion and summary

This chapter has attempted to provide an explanatory adequacy with English data, exhibiting how determiners and prenominal modifiers are ordered relying on Haiman's distance principle, in particular, the explanation of the order of multiple determiners or multiple adjectives. The results have verified that the ordering of English prenominal modifiers can be identified in terms of the distance principle on the condition that the proper motivating factors governing the prenominal modifiers can be found. The significant findings of the section are generalized and restated below so that a clearer view towards the ordering of determiners and prenominal modifiers will be provided.

First of all, determiners tend to precede the other prenominal modifiers and stay distant from the head noun for the reason that determiners, having the identifying or quantifying function, mainly embody the semantic features extrinsic to the head noun but pointing to the relation with communicative context. Unlike the determiners that are conceptually distant from the head noun, the other prenominal modifiers, bearing the qualifying function, satisfy the intrinsic semantic information of the head noun and thus bear the qualifying function from a perspective of discourse analysis. Among a noun phrase, a bundle of determiners mostly bear the order following the principle given in the statement (139) below:

(139) The order of determiners within a noun phrase:

generic quantifiers > identifying determiners > numerals > HEAD NOUN

Numerals are regarded as the specific quantifying feature of the head noun, while identifying determiner can only make the head noun syntactically a definite or referential entity. Generic quantifiers precede identifying determiners for the reason that they are totally parasitic on identifying determiners. As far as generic determiners are concerned, linguistic distance varies depending on the obligatoriness/optionality of the "of-insertion" in between. Based on the three conditions for the "of-insertion" to license determiner combinations, two determinant factors can interpret the linguistic distance of generic quantifiers to the head noun: the part-and-whole relation and multipliability between the part and whole.

Among the prenominal modifiers, supporting evidence is gained based on Quirk's criteria of judging the semantic properties of adjectives. Both explanation and data confirm one fact: when they serve as modifiers within a nominal phrase, nouns and gerunds are always positioned closest to the head noun. Relying on Haiman's conceptual closeness, linguistic closeness reflects conceptual closeness which in turn implies the similar semantic properties between them. Judging from Quirk's criteria of semantic properties, linguistic closeness between the head and the gerund reflects their syntactic closeness in speaker's conceptualizing process. That is, when a noun or a gerund premodifies its head, it exhibits more noun-like semantic properties than other modifiers do, and in syntactical form, they are arranged close to each other, while a further analysis of (past and present) participles reveals that they are distant from the head noun because they remain more or less their original verbal semantic properties. This kind of distance principle can be summarized into what is called "The Principle of Nouniness", shown below:

(140) a. The more nominal properties a prenominal modifier has, the closer to the head;
b. the more adjective properties a prenominal modifier has, the less close to the head;
c. the more verbal properties a prenominal modifier has, the least close to the head.

In terms of this principle, the general prenominal modifier order can be established as follows:

(141) (Past and Present) Participles > Adjectives > Denominal Adjectives > Nouns > Gerunds > HEAD NOUN

Adjectives, taking up a majority of prenominal modifiers, cannot be ignored because of the prominent feature of being (un)gradable. However, a single polarity of being gradable/ungradable is not sufficient enough to be a criterion to order all types of adjectives. This study carefully selects six calibrations to carry out a notion of gradability degree of adjectives. The six calibrations are all based on the semantic properties of adjectives. They are subjectivity, relativity, cultural variations, continuity, immeasurability and non-prototype. The six calibrations help to specify the original gradable polarity. The gradability degree of each adjective will be evaluated by how many calibrations they observe. The more calibrations they follow up, the higher in the gradability degree they are, the more distant they are from the head, and vice versa. This study also takes exemplifications to illustrate how to perform the gradability degree. It aims to prove that the degree of gradability of adjectives is closely related to the ordering of prenominal adjectives in English. In terms of the gradability degrees, the gradable/ungradable polarity is no longer transmitted abruptly because gradability degree is aimed to judge how many properties each adjective has. We intend to gain much clearer comprehension of the distinction between adjectives by means of quantitative study of various adjective features. Related to the distance principle again, our findings are generalized as follows:

(142) Judged from the six calibrations on the gardability level,

a. the lower a prenominal adjective is in the gradability degree, the closer to the head noun;

b. the higher a prenominal adjective in the gradability degree, the furthest to the head noun.

In this way, the present chapter can be concluded: the orders of both determiners and prenominal modifiers are not arbitrary but motivated by certain factors. These factors can be interpreted by either their functions or their semantic properties. Relating these determinant factors to the distance principle, the rule of ordering determiners and modifiers has clearly been identified.

CHAPTER SIX CONCLUSION

Throughout the research, thanks to iconicity principles, an investigation of word order within a noun phrase has been presented. This chapter will first summarize all the findings, then point out the limitations of the present research, and finally propose possible avenues of further work.

6.1. Findings

First, a large number of researchers have benefited from iconicity principles to solve those central syntactic problems. This research is an important step in inviting word order within a noun phrase, being a member of the peripheral family in language, to a position equal to the central ones. The results, too, are as convincing and significant as what is expected. That is, word order phenomena within a noun phrase belong to the whole theory of sign in that it shares many properties with some other systems of signs. It is a hope that this research will inspire more researchers to utilize iconic approach for the discovery of language natures to solve those peripheral problems in language.

Second, the efforts to analyze both English and Chinese coordinate idioms can support the fact that their orders are not arbitrarily fixed or frozen.

On account of the temporal and spatial order shown in substantial English and Chinese data, a conclusion can be drawn that both Chinese and English coordinate idioms are to a considerable extent iconic of the spatial and temporal sequence in the natural or the experiential world. The orders of the conjuncts in these coordinate idioms are exactly the reflections of human concepts and experience from the real world.

Dealing with the sequence of coordinate idioms by means of unmarked-marked and positive-negative order verifies that the polarity-driven and markedness-based orders can be in the same way explained by iconicity principles for the same reason that they are essentially motivated by human bodily embodiment and cognitive abilities.

It further verifies that Birdsong's (1995) assumption that the respective roles of markedness, cognitive constraints and iconicity are thought as independent or exclusive of one another, is not the case at all. Instead, the results have manifested that both markedness and cognitive constraints can be incorporated into iconicity because one point is very salient in both English and Chinese: the expression orders follow human perceptual or cognitive abilities. No matter whether it is marked or positive, it is conceptually oriented and experiencedly iconic. This is compatible with the sequential order principle: the linear sequence of linguistic structures iconically corresponds to the conceptual order it represents.

Third, an explanation with English data has been made on how the determiners and the other prenominal modifiers are ordered. The close observation to the data demonstrates that the ordering of English prenominal modifiers can be explained in terms of the distance principle on the condition that the appropriate motivating factors governing the prenominal modifiers can be found. Due to the complexity of prenominal modifiers in English, this research has separated the analysis processes into three domains: determiners, adjectival prenominal modifiers and prenominal adjectives.

As far as all the determiners are concerned, they tend to precede the other prenominal modifiers and take the position distant from the head noun for the reason that determiners, merely having the identifying or quantifying function, mostly embody the semantic features extrinsic to the head noun but pointing to the relation with communicative context. They are conceptually less intimate with the head noun, while the remaining prenominal modifiers, having the qualifying function, satisfy the intrinsic semantic information of the head noun. The order among determiners within a noun phrase is further to be considered as: "generic quantifiers > identifying determiners > numerals > ... > the head noun". Numerals are regarded as an intrinsic feature of the head noun, while an identifying determiner can only make the head noun syntactically a definite or referential entity. Generic quantifiers precede identifying determiners for the reason that they are totally parasitic on the identifying determiners.

As for generic determiners, linguistic distance varies depending on the obligatoriness/optionality of the "*of*"-insertion in between. Based on the three revised conditions for the "*of*"-insertion to license determiner combinations, two determinants help to interpret the linguistic distance of generic quantifiers to the head noun: the part-and-whole relation and multipliability between the part and whole.

Among adjectival prenominal modifiers, supporting evidence is gained from Quirk et al's (1972) criteria of judging the semantic properties of adjectives. Both explanation and data confirm one fact: when nouns and gerunds serve as modifiers, they stay closest to the head noun. Relying on Haiman's (1985a) conceptual closeness, linguistic closeness reflects conceptual closeness which in turn implies the similar semantic properties between them. Grounded on Quirk et al's (1972) criteria for adjective semantic properties, our detailed examination further proves that linguistic closeness between noun (gerund) modifier and the head noun reflects their semantic similarity. That is, when a noun or a gerund premodifies its head, it will exhibit more noun-like semantic properties than other modifiers do. While a further analysis of (past and present) participles reveals that they are distant from the head noun because they remain more or less their original verbal semantic properties. The statements can be summarized into what is named "The Principle of Nouniness", which is stated as follows:

a. The more nominal properties a prenominal modifier has, the closer to the head noun;

b. The more adjectival properties a prenominal modifier has, the less close to the head;

c. The more verbal properties a prenominal modifier has, the least close to the head.

In light of this principle, the general order of adjectival prenominal modifiers can be established as follows:

(Past and Present) Participles > Adjectives > Denominal Adjectives > Nouns > Gerunds > HEAD NOUN

Adjectives, as the core member of prenominal modifiers, can never be neglected owing to their prominent features of being modifiers. However, a single polarity of being gradable/ungradable is not sufficient enough to be a criterion to order all types of adjectives. This study carefully selects six calibrations to carry out a notion of gradability degree of adjectives: subjectivity, relativity, cultural variations, continuity, immeasurability and non-prototype. The six calibrations help to specify the original gradable polarity. The gradability degree of each adjective will be evaluated by how many calibrations they obey. The more calibrations they obey, the higher in the gradability degree they are, the more distant they are from the head, and vice versa. This study also takes exemplifications to illustrate how to perform the gradability degree. It aims to prove that the degree of gradability of adjectives is closely related to the ordering of prenominal adjectives in English.

In terms of the gradability degrees, the gradable/ungradable polarity is no longer transmitted abruptly because gradability degree is aimed to judge how many properties each adjective has. We intend to gain much clearer comprehension of the distinction between adjectives by means of quantitative study of various adjective features. Related to the distance principle again, our findings are generalized below:

Judged from the six calibrations on the gardability level,

a. the lower a prenominal adjective is in the gradability degrees, the closer to the head noun;

b. the higher a prenominal adjective is in the gradability degrees, the more distant to the head noun.

Fourth, from a perspective of a researcher or language teacher of English, this cognition-based analysis approach facilitates a better position to tackle some unique phenomena demonstrated in foreign language teaching. For instance, given the sample physical situation where "*many books in the library*", the preferred responses from English and Chinese speaking people in their verbal descriptions are distinctive, though alternative patterns are available in both languages. In English, we have two patterns corresponding to this situation:

(143) a. There are many books in the library.

b. The library has many books.

In Chinese, we have the following two sentences:

(144) a. 有 很多 书 在 图书馆 里。

"have-V many-MOD books-Obj in-Prep the library-Obj."

b. 图书馆 里 有 很多 书。

"library-Subj in-Prep have-V many-MOD books-Obj."

Any English native speaker can choose (143a) as the preferred pattern, while Chinese speakers would favor (144b). But why is it the case? How should we explain the phenomenon of different preference to students?

Since both languages allow both patterns, the difference seems not to be a matter of absoluteness, but a matter of the preference to look at the same situation. An exploration into cognitive linguistics is helpful to find an easier construal for these grammar problems. It will be clear that the preference of (144b) over (144a) in Chinese is due to the fact that Whole-Before-Part is the most preferred Chinese word order in the topic of locations, while the opposite are the English speakers.

From a pedagogical perspective, the cognition-based approach will better our position in dealing with problems as such in the teaching of the target language on its own terms. As has been shown in this study, the illustrated Chinese preference is due to the impact of some predominant conceptual structures in Chinese, and can be accounted for by the cognition-based approach, which provides us with a different angle to approach universals across languages as well as features unique to individual languages. A linguistic study with this approach will contribute an explanatory means to the ever-demanding requirements in the foreign language teaching to help both teachers and students better teach and grasp the target language in terms of the conceptual system of different languages. It is from this pedagogical perspective that I would focus on word order phenomena, which can be explained in terms of iconicity principles.

6.2. Limitations and further work

It is self-evident that due to the pervasive permeability of language in human social life, there are simply many factors motivating the order of syntactic constructions, but too many to cover individually within the limited space of this study. For the research purposes, merely the iconicity principles are adopted since this research is most interested in observing the order phenomena at the phrasal level independent of the discourse context. Indeed, other principles such as information structure, pragmatic maxims and conventional factors may improve the results.

I have explored the word order within a noun phrase and their relations to the variety of iconic or cognitive factors. Although my goal of solving these problems seemed manageable enough at first glance, I am often trapped by some of the exceptions that confront me. I tend to explain them phonologically, historically or conventionally. This might decrease the explanatory adequacy of iconicity principles. Currently, I believe that the study of word order within a noun phrase touches on matters that extend to a variety of both linguistic and cognitive issues. Deeper considerations into those problems may be helpful and possible to find the answer. However, sometimes I am satisfied with passively borrowing the theories that are well-explained by the literatures. If an optimistic attitude is developed to actively seek for new points of view, the findings will be more creative or original.

In the investigation of the gradability level of prenominal adjectives referring to the shape and color, disagreement arises when adjectives concerning color terms are juxtaposed with adjectives referring to shapes. Because of the complexity of the nature of color terms, it is difficult for us to make an objective evaluation of the values of their gradability. Thus I turn to the explanation of idiomatic usage to seek for the solution. Indeed, there should exist a cognitive explanation behind this complex phenomenon. We can consider it as our further work to be an extension of this work.

At last, it should be clearly stated that iconicity principles are only a general theoretical tendency. It never means to deny the existence of other competing motivations in language. This disadvantage is expectable in that iconicity principles, at its developing stage, need to be extended, rather than totally expelled. Researchers can consider the further task of ascertaining and implementing a comprehensive iconic system.

References

Allan, K. 1987. Hierarchies and the choice of left conjuncts (with particular attention to English). *Journal of Linguistics* 23(1), 51 – 77.

Allott, R. 1995. Motor Theory of Language in Relation to Syntax. M. E. Landsberg (ed.). *Syntactic Iconicity and Linguistic Freezes.* Berlin: Mouton de Gruyter.

Anderson, E. R. 1998. *A Grammar of Iconism.* London: Faircleigh Dickinson University Associated University Press.

Anttila, R. 1989. *Historical and Comparative Linguistics.* Amsterdam: John Benjamins.

Anttila, R. and S. Embleton. 1994. The Iconic Index: From Sound Change to Rhyming Slang. R. Simone (ed.). *Iconicity in Language.* Amsterdam: John Benjamins.

Bache, C. 1978. *The Order of Premodifying Adjectives in Present-Day English.* Odense: Odense University.

Bailey, C. J. N. and R. Harris (eds.). 1985. *Development Mechanisms of Language.* Oxford: Pergamon Press.

Baker, M. 1988. *Incorporation: A Theory of Grammatical Function Change.* Chicago: University of Chicago Press.

Bates, E. and B. MacWhinney. 1978. Sentential devices for conveying givenness and newness: A cross-cultural developmental study. *Journal of Verbal Learning and*

Verbal Behavior 17 (5), 539 – 558.

Bates, E. and B. MacWhinney. 1981. Second Language Aquisition from a Functionalis Perspective: Pragmatic, Semantic and Perceptual Strategies. W. Henry (ed.). *Annuals of the New York Academy of Sciences Conference on Native and Foreign Language Acquisition*, vol. 379, 190 – 214. New York: New York Academy of Sciences.

Bates, E. and B. MacWhinney. 1982. Functionalist Approaches to Grammar. E. Wanner and L. Gleitman (eds.). *Language Acquisition: The State of the Art*, 173 – 218. Cambridge: Cambridge University Press.

Bates, E. and B. MacWhinney. 1989. Functionalism and the Competition Model. MacWhinney B. and E. Bates (eds.). *The Cross-linguistic Study of Sentence Processing*. Cambridge: Cambridge University Press.

Behagel, O. 1932. *Deutsche Syntax: Eine geschichtliche Darstellung*, vol. 4, Wortstellung: Periodendau. Heidelberg: Carl Winters Universt tsbechhandlung.

Berlin, B. and P. Kay. 1969. *Basic Color Terms: Their Universality and Evolution*. Berkeley: University of California Press.

Birdsong, D. 1995. Iconicity, Markedness and Processing Constraints in Frozen Locution. M. E. Landsberg (ed.). *Syntactic Iconicity and Linguistic Freezes*, 31 – 45. Berlin: Mouton de Gruyter.

Bloomfield, L. 2002. *Language*. Beijing: Foreign Language Teaching and Research Press.

Bolinger, D. 1975. *Aspects of Language* (2nd edition). New York: Harcount, Brace, Jovanovich.

Bolinger, D. 1977. *Meaning and Form*. London: Longman.

Bolinger, D and D. A. Sears. 1981. *Aspects of Language*. New York: Harcourt Brace Jovanovich.

Bouissac, P. (ed.). 1998. *Encyclopedia of Semiotics*. Oxford: Oxford University Press.

Brown, K. and J. Miller. 1991. *Syntax: A Linguistic Introduction to Sentence Structure.* London: Routledge.

Bybee, J. L. 1985. Diagrammatic Iconicity in Stem-inflection Relations. Haiman, J. (ed.). *Iconicity in Syntax*, 1 – 11. Amsterdam: John Benjamins.

Chafe, W. 1970. *Meaning and the Structure of Language.* Chicago: University of Chicago Press.

Chafe, W. 1976. Givenness, Contrastiveness, Definiteness, Subject, Topic and Point of View. Li, C. N. (ed.). *Word Order and Word Order Change*, 25 – 55. Austin: University of Texas Press.

Chafe, W. and J. Nichols. 1986. *Evidentiality: The Linguistic Coding of Epistemology.* Norwood, N. J.: Ablex.

Chandler, D. 2002. *Semiotics: The Basics.* London: Routledge.

Chao, Y. R. 1968. *A Grammar of Spoken Chinese.* Berkeley: University of California Press.

Chomsky, N. 1965. *Aspects of the Theory of Syntax.* Cambridge, Massachusetts: M. I. T. Press.

Chomsky, N. 1972. *Language and Mind (2nd edition)*. New York: Harcourt, Brace, Jovanovich.

Chomsky, N. 1973. Conditions on Transformation. S. Anderson and R. Kiparsky (eds.). *A Festschrift for Morris Halle.* New York: Holt, Rinehar and Winston.

Chomsky, N. 1980. *Rules and Representations.* New York: Columbia University Press.

Chomsky, N. 1981. On the representation of form and function. *The Linguistic Review* 1(1), 3 – 40.

Christina L. 2001. Iconic Dimensions in Margaret Atwood's Poetry and Prose. M. Nanny and O. Fischer (eds.). *The Motivated Sign — Iconicity in Language and Literature* 2. Amsterdam: John Benjamins.

Clark, H. H. 1973. Space, Time, Semantics and the Child. Moore (ed.). *Cognitive Development and the Acquisition of Language*, 28 – 64. New York: Academic Press.

Clark, H. H. and W. G. Chase. 1974. Perceptual Coding Strategies in the Formation and Verification of Descriptions. *Memory and Cognition* 2(1), 101 – 111.

Clark, A. and A. D. B. Clark. (eds.). 1974. *Mental Deficiency, the Changing Outlook.* New York: Macmillan.

Cooper, W. E. and J. R. Ross. 1975. Word Order. R. E. Grossman et al (eds.). *Papers from the Parasession on Functionalism*, 63 – 111. Chicago: Chicago Linguistic Society.

Conradie, C. J. 2001. Structural Iconicity: The English S-and OF-genitives. M. Nanny and O. Fischer (eds.). *The Motivated Sign — Iconicity in Language and Literature* 2, 230 – 248. Amsterdam: John Benjamins.

Cowan, Ron. 1995. What are Discourse Principles Made of. P. Downing and M. Noonan (eds.). *Word Order in Discourse.* Amsterdam: John Benjamins.

Creider, C. 1977. Functional Sentence Perspective in a Verb-initial Language . Kotey P. F. and H. Der-Houssikian (eds.). *Language and Linguistic Problems in Africa*, 330 – 343. Columbia, S. C. : Hornbeam Press,

Croft, W. 1990. *Typology and Universals.* Cambridge: Cambridge University Press.

Croft, W. 2000. *Typology and Universals.* Beijing: Foreign Language Teaching and Research Press.

Croft, W. and D. A. Cruse. 2004. *Cognitive Linguistics.* Cambridge: Cambridge University Press.

Crowell, T. L. 1964. *Index to Modern English.* New York: McGraw-Hill.

Cruse, D. A. 1990. Prototype Theory and Lexical Semantics. Tsohatzidis, S. L. (ed.). *Meaning and Prototype*, 382 – 402. London: Routledge.

Danes, F. 1974. Functional Sentence Perspective and the Organization of the Text. F. Danes (ed.). *Papers on Functional Sentence Perspective*, 106 – 128. Hague, Paris: Mouton

de Beaugrande, R. and W. Dressler. 1981. *Introduction to Text Linguistics*. London and New York: Longman.

de Schutter, G. 1987. Pragmatic Positions: The Case of Modifying Clauses in Dutch. J. Nuyts and G. de Schutter (eds.). *Getting One's Words into Line: On Word Order and Functional Grammar*, 103 – 118. Dordrecht, Holland, Providence, R. I.

Diehl, Lon. 1975. Space Case: 'Some Principles and Their Implications Concerning Linear Order in Natural Languages'. *Working Papers of the Summer Institute of Linguistics, University of North Dakota Session* 19, 93 – 150.

Dik, S. C. 1978. *Functional Grammar*. Amsterdam: North Holland Publishing Company.

Dixon, R. M. W. 1982. *Where Have All the Adjectives Gone?* Berlin: Mouton Publisher.

Dixon, R. 1991. *A New Approach to English Grammar on Semantic Principles*. Oxford: Clarendon Press.

Dotter, F. 1995. Nonarbitrariness and Iconicity: Coding Possibility. M. E. Landsberg (ed.). *Syntactic Iconicity and Linguistic Freezes*. Berlin: Mouton de Gruyter.

Downing, P. and M. Noonan (eds.). 1995. *Word Order in Discourse*. Amsterdam: John Benjamins.

Dressler, W. U. Mayerthaler, W. and O. Panagl. 1987. Referring and accessibility. *Journal of Linguistics* 24 (1), 65 – 87.

Dryer, M. S. 1984. A Statistical Study of Word Order Universals. *Final Report for Social Science and Humanities Research Council of Canada*.

Du Bois, J. 1985. Competing Motivation. J. Haiman (ed.). *Iconicity in Syntax*,

343 – 365. Amsterdam: John Benjamins.

Edmondson, J. A. 1985. Biological Foundations of Language Universals. C. J. N. Bailey and R. Harris. (eds.). *Developmental Mechanism of Language*, 109 – 130. Oxford: Pergamon Press.

Enkvist, N. E. 1981. Experiential iconicism in text strategy. *Text*, 1(1): 97 – 111.

Enkvist, N. E. 1989. Connexity, Interpretability, Universes of Discourse, and Text Worlds. S. Allen (ed.). *Possible Worlds in Humanities, Arts and Sciences*, 162 – 186. Berlin/New York: Water de Gruyter.

Fischer, O. 1999. On the Role Played by Iconicity in Grammaticalization Processes. M. Nanny and O. Fischer (eds.). *Form Miming Meaning — Iconicity in Language and Literature*, 345 – 374. Amsterdam: John Benjamins.

Fischer, O. 2001. The Position of the Adjective in (Old) English from an Iconic Perspective. F. Olga and M. Nanny (eds.). *The Motivated Sign*, 249 – 276. Amsterdan: John Benjamins.

Firbas, J. 1964. On Defining the Theme in Functional Sentence Analysis. *Travaux Linguistiques de Prague* 1: 267 – 80.

Firbas, J. 1992. *Functional Sentence Perspective in Written and Spoken Communication.* Cambridge: Cambridge University Press.

Foley, W. and R. van Valin. 1984. *Functional Syntax and Universal Grammar.* Cambridge: Cambridge University Press.

Foley, W. A. 2000. *Anthropological Linguistics: An Introduction.* Beijing: Foreign Language Teaching and Research Press.

Fowler, H. W. 2003. *A Dictionary of Modern English Usage.* Oxford: Oxford University Press. (Originally published in 1926.)

Frawley, W. 1992. *Linguistic Semantics.* Lawrence Erlbaum Associates, Hillsdale, New Jersey.

Feist, J. 2009. Premodifier order in English nominal phrases: A semantic account. *Cognitive Linguistics*, 20(2), 301 -340.

Gensini, S. 1994. Criticism of the Arbitrariness of Language in Leibniz and the 'Natural' Philosophy of Language. R. Simone (ed.). *Iconicity in Language*. Amsterdam; Philadelphia: John Benjamins.

Givón, T. 1979. *On Understanding Grammar*. New York: Academic Press.

Givón, T. 1984. Direct Object and Dative Shifting: Semantic and Pragmatic Case. F. Plank (ed.). *Objects*, 151 -182. London: Academic Press.

Givón, T. 1985. Iconicity, Isomorphism, and Non-arbitrary Coding in Syntax. J. Haiman (ed.). *Iconicity in Syntax*, 187 -219. Amsterdam: John Benjamins.

Givón, T. 1990. *Syntax: A Functional-Typological Introduction*. vol. II, Amsterdam: John Benjamins.

Givón, T. 1991. Isomorphism in the grammatical code: Cognitive and biological considerations. *Studies in Language* 15 (1), 85 -114.

Givón, T. 1993. *English Grammar*. Amsterdam: John Benjamins.

Givón, T. 1994. Isomorphism in the Grammatical Code: Cognitive and Biological Considerations. R. Simone (ed.). *Iconicity in Language*: 47 -76. Amsterdam: John Benjamins.

Givón, T. 1995. Markedness as Meta-iconicity: Distributional and Cognitive Correlates of Syntactic Structure. T. Givón. *Functionalism and Grammar*, 25 -69. Amsterdam: John Benjamins.

Goyvaerts, D. L. 1968. An introductory study on the ordering of a string of adjectives in present-day English. *Philologica Pragensia*, 11, 12 -28.

Green, G. 1974. *Semantics and Syntactic Regularity*. Bloomington, IN: Indiana University Press.

Greenberg, J. H. 1963. Some Universals of Language with Special Reference to the Order of Meaningful Elements. J. H. Greenberg (ed.). *Universals of Language*,

58 – 90. MA :MIT Press.

Greenberg, J. H. (ed.). 1966. *Universals of Language.* MA: MIT Press.

Greenberg, J. H. 1995. On Language and Internal Iconicity. M. E. Landsberg (ed.). *Syntactic Iconicity and Linguistic Freezes.* Berlin: Mouton de Gruyter.

Haiman, J. 1980. The iconicity of grammar: Isomorphim and motivation. *Language* 56(3), 515 – 540.

Haiman, J. 1983. Iconic and economic motivation. *Language* 59(4), 781 – 819.

Haiman, J. 1985a. *Natural Syntax-Iconicity and Erosion.* Cambridge: Cambridge University Press.

Haiman, J. (ed.). 1985b. *Iconicity in Syntax.* Amsterdam: John Benjamins.

Hale, K. 1981. *On the Position of Walbiri in a Typology of the Base.* Mimeo: MIT Press.

Hawkins, J. A. 1983. *Word Order Universal.* London: Academic Press.

Halliday, M. A. K., 1985. Dimensions of Discourse Analysis: Grammar. T. A. van Dijk (ed.). *Handbook of Discourse Analysis, Vol. 2: Dimensions of Discourse.* London: Academic Press.

Halliday, M. A. K. 2000. *An Introduction to Functional Grammar.* Beijing: Foreign Language and Teaching Research Press.

Heider, K. G. 1970. *The Dugum Dani.* Chicago: Aldine Publishing Co.

Heider, E. Rosch. 1971. Focal color areas and the development of color names. *Developmental Psychology* 4 (3), 447 – 455.

Heine, B. 1997. *Possession: Cognitive Sources, Forces and Grammaticalization.* Cambridge: Cambridge University Press.

Hetzron, R. 1978. *On the Relative Order of Adjectives.* H. Seiler (ed.). *Language Universals*, 165 – 184, Tübingen: Narr.

Hockett, C. F. 1958. *A Course in Modern Linguistics.* Newyork: Macmillan.

Hörmann, H. 1971. *Psycholinguistics: An Introduction to Research and Theory.*

Berlin: Springer-Verlag.

Hopper, P and S. Thompson. 1980. Transitivity in grammar and discourse. *Language* 56, 29 – 87.

Huddleston, R. 1984. *Introduction to the Grammar of English*. Cambridge: Cambridge University Press.

Humboldt, W. V. 1988. *On Language: The Diversity of Human Language Structure and its Influence on the Mental Development of Mankind*. (Trans.) by Peter Health. Cambridge: Cambridge University Press.

Hwang, Kyu-Hong. 2004. An iconicity-theoretic approach to argument structure alternations in English. *Journal of Language Science* 2(1), 251 – 271.

Hyman, L. and Hawkinson, A. 1975. Hierarchies of natural topic in shona. *Studies in African Linguistics* 5 (2), 147 – 170.

Itkonen, E. 2004. Typological explanation and iconicity. *Logos and Language* 5 (1), 21 – 33.

Jakobson, R. 1962. *Selected Writings III*. The Hague: Mouton.

Jakobson, R. 1971a. Quest for the Essence of Language. R. Jakobson (ed.). *Selected Writings* vol. II, 345 – 59. The Hague: Mouton. [Originally published in Diogenes 51 (1966)].

Jakobson, R. 1971b. Language in Relation to Other Communication Systems. R. Jakobson (ed.). *Selected Writings*. The Hague: Mouton.

Jakobson, R. 1975. Concluding Statement: Linguistics and Poetics. T. A. Sebeok (ed.). *Style in Language*, 350 – 377. MA: MIT Press.

Jellinek, H. M. 1913 – 14. *Geschichte der Neuhochdeutschen Grammatik von den AnFangenbis auf Adelung*. Heidelberg: Winter.

Jespersen, Otto. 1949. *A Modern English Grammar on Historical Principles*. Vol. vii. London: George Allen and Unwin.

Johnson-Llaird, P. N. 1983. The Coherence of Discourse. P. N. Johnson-Llaird (ed.). *Mental Models*, 233 – 274. Cambridge: Cambridge University of Press.

Kay, P. and C. McDaniel. 1978. The linguistic significance of the meanings of color terms. *Language* 54(3), 610 – 646.

Kim, Doo-Shick. 1999. *A Discourse-functional Analysis of Subject-verb Inversion in English.* Seoul: Hankuk Publisher.

Kim, Doo-Shick. 2007a. *New University English Grammar.* JinJu: Gyeongsang National University.

Kim, Doo-Shick. 2007b. *The Ordering and Combinational Restrictions on English Determinatives.* JinJu: Gyeongsang National University.

Kintsch, W. and A. Van Dijk. 1978. Towards a model of text comprehension and production. *Psychological Review* 84(5), 363 – 394.

Kortmann, B. 1999. Iconicity, Typology and Cognition. M. Nanny and O. Fischer (eds.). *Form Miming Meaning — Iconicity in Language and Literature.* Amsterdam: John Benjamins.

Krupa, Viktor. 1982. *Languages of Asia and Africa. Vol 4: The Polynesian Languages.* London: Routledge and Kegan Paul.

Kuh, Hakan. 1990. *Correlation between Inflection and Word Order.* Doctoral Dissertation. The Ohio State University.

Lakoff, G. and M. Johnson. 1980. *Metaphors We Live By.* Chicago: Chicago University Press.

Lakoff, G. and M. Johnson. 1987. *Women, Fire and Dangerous Things: What Categories Reveal about the Mind.* Chicago: The University of Chicago Press.

Lakoff, G. 1991. Cognitive versus generative linguistics: Who commitments influence results. *Language and Communication* 11(1 – 2), 53 – 62.

Lambrecht, K. 1984. Formulaicity, frame semantics and german binominal expressions. *Language* 60(4), 753 – 96.

Landsberg, M. E. 1987. Semantic Aspects of Syntactic Iconicity. R. Crespo et al

(eds.). *Aspects of Language*, vol 2, 233 – 247.

Landsberg, M. E. (ed.). 1995. *Syntactic Iconicity and Linguistic Freezes*. Berlin: Mouton de Gruyter.

Langacker, R, W. 1987a. Nouns and verbs. *Language* 63(1), 53 – 94.

Langacker, R, W. 1987b. *Foundations of Cognitive Grammar vol. I: Theoretical Prerequisites*. Stanford: Stanford University Press.

Langacker, R. W. 1991a. *Foundations of Cognitive Grammar*. Stanford: Stanford University Press.

Langacker, R. W. 1991b. *Concept, Image, and Symbol: The Cognitive Basis of Grammar*. New York, Mouton de Gruyter.

Langacker, R. W. 1993. Reference-point constructions. *Cognitive Linguistics*, 4 (1):1 – 38.

Leibniz, G. W. 1981. *New Essays on Human Understanding*. Translated and edited by Peter remnant and Jonathan Bennett. Cambridge: Cambridge University Press.

Lehrer, A. 1985. Markedness and antonymy. *Journal of Linguistics* 31 (3), 397 – 429.

Li, Charles. N. 1976. *Word Order and Word order Change*. Austin: University of Texas Press.

Li, Charles N. and S. A. Thompson. 1973. Serial verb constructions in mandarin Chinese. Papers from the Comparative Syntax Festival, Chicago Linguistics Society, 96 – 103.

Li, Charles N. and S. A. Thompson. 1975. The Semantic Function of Word Order in Chinese. Charles N. Li (ed.). *Word Order and Word Order Change*. Austin: University of Texas Press.

Li, Charles N. and S. A. Thompson. 1976. Subject and Topic: A New Typology of Language. Charles N. Li (ed.). *Subject and Topic*, 457 – 489. New York: Academic Press.

Lin, Lu. 2007. Experiential iconicity in discourse. *The Journal of Modern British and American Language and Literature* 25(2), 33 -48.

Locke, J. 1994. *An Essay Concerning Human Understanding*. Abridged and edited by W. John. Yolton London: Everyman.

Lyons, G. 1979. *Semantics*. Cambridge: Cambridge University Press.

Malkiel, Yakov. 1959. Studies in irreversible binomials. *Lingua* 8(2), 113 -160.

Malkiel, Yakov. 1968. *Essays on Linguistic Themes*. Blackwell, Oxford.

Mallison, G. and B. Blake. 1981. *Language Typology*. Amsterdam: North Holland.

Masako, K. Hiraga. 1998. Metaphor-icon link in poetic texts: A cognitive approach to iconicity. *The Journal of the University of the Air* 16, 147 -176.

Mathesius, V. 1975. A Functional Analysis of Present-day English on a General Linguistic Basis. Trans. by Josef Vachek. Libuše Duškovά Prague: Academia.

Mayerthaler, Willi. 1981. *Morphologische Naturlichkeit*. Wiesbaden. Athenaion.

Meillet, A. 1970. *The Comparative Method in Historical Linguistics*. Trans. by B. Gordon and J. R. Ford. Paris: Librairie Honore Champion, edjieur.

Merrel, F. 1999. Charles Sander Peirce's Concept of the Sign. P. Cobley(ed.). *Semiotics and Linguisitcs*, 28 -39 London: Routledge.

Mithun, M. 1995. Morphological and Prosodic Forces Shaping Word Order. Downing, P. and M. Noonan (eds.). *Word Order in Discourse*, 387 -423. Amsterdam: John Benjamins.

Müller, W. G. 1999. The Iconic Use of Syntax in British and American Fiction. M. Nanny and O. Fischer (eds.). *Form Miming Meaning — Iconicity in Language and Literature*, 214 -235. Amsterdam: John Benjamins.

Nanny, M. and O. Fischer (eds.). 1999. *Form Miming Meaning — Iconicity in Language and Literature*. Amsterdam: John Benjamins.

Nanny, M. and O. Fischer (eds.). 2001. *The Motivated Sign — Iconicity in Language and Literature* 2. Amsterdam: John Benjamins.

Newmeyer, F. J. 1998a. The irrelevance of typology for grammatical theory. *Syntaxis* 1, 161 – 197.

Newmeyer, F. J. 1998b. *Language Form and Language Function.* Cambridge, MA: MTT Press.

Norrman, R. 1999. Creating the World in our Image: A New Theory of Love of Symmetry and Iconicist Desire. M. Nanny and O. Fischer (eds.). *Form Miming Meaning — Iconicity in Language and Literature*, 59 – 82. Amsterdam: John Benjamins.

Nöth, W. 1999. Peircian Semiotics in the Study of Iconicity in Language. *Transactions of the Charles S. Peirce Society Summer*, *Vol XXXV*, *No.* 3.

Nöth, W. 2001. Semiotic Foundations of Iconicity in Language and Literature. M. Nanny and O. Fischer (eds.). *The Motivated Sign — Iconicity in Language and Literature* 2, 18 – 27. Amsterdam: John Benjamins.

Nunberg, G. Ivan, A. Sag and W. Thomas. 1994. Idioms. *Language* 70 (3), 491 – 538.

Nuyts, J. and G. de Schutter (eds.). 1987. *Getting One's Words into Line: On Word Order and Functional Grammar.* Dordrecht, Holland, Providence, R. I.

Payne, D. L. (ed.). 1992. *Pragmatics of Word Order Flexibility.* Amsterdam: John Benjamins.

Payne, D. L. 1995. Verb Initial Languages and Information Order. Downing, P. and M. Noonan (eds.). *Word Order in Discourse.* Amsterdam: John Benjamins.

Peirce, C. S. 1940. *The Philosophy of C. S. Peirce.* J. Buchler (ed.). New York: Harcourt, Brace and Jovanovich.

Peirce, C. S. 1955. Logic and Semiotic: Theory of Signs. J. Buchler (ed.). *Philosophical Writings* 98 – 119. New York: Dover.

Pinker, S. and D. Birdsong. 1979. Speakers' sensitivity to rules of frozen word order. *Journal of Verbal Learning and Verbal Behavior* 18(4), 497 - 508.

Pinker, S. 1989. *Learnability and Cognition: The Acquisition of Argument Structure.* MA: the MIT Press.

Plank, Frans. 1979. Ikonisierung und De-Ikonisierung als Prinzipien des Sprachwandels. Spraychwissenschaft 4, 121 - 158.

Plato. 1926. *Cratylus. Plato, Vol. IV.* H. N. Fowler (trans.). London: William Heinemann.

Pullum, G. 1981. Language with object before subject: A comment and a catalogue. *Linguistics.* 19(1 - 2):147 - 156.

Quirk, R. Greenbaum, S. Leech, G. and Jan Svartvik. 1972. *A Comprehensive Grammar of the English Language.* London: Longman.

Quirk, R. Greenbaum, S. Leech, G. and Jan Svartvik. 1985. *A Comprehensive Grammar of the English Language.* New York: Longman.

Ransom, E. N. 1979. Definiteness and animacy constraints on passive and double-object constructions in English. *Glossa* 13, 215 - 240.

Rosch, E. 1978. Principles of Categorization. E. Rosch and B. B. Lloyd (eds.). *Cognition and Categorization*, 27 - 48. Erlbaum.

Ross. D. A. 1973. Nouniness. *Three Dimensions of Linguistic Research.* Osamu Fujimora.

Sadowski, P. 2001. The Sound as an Echo to the Sense: The Iconicity of English *gl-w*ords. F. Olga and M. Nanny (eds.). *The Motivated Sign*, 69 - 88. Amsterdam, John Benjamins.

Saeed, J. 1997. *Semantics.* Oxford: Blackwell.

Sapir, E. 2001. *Language.* Beijing: Foreign Language Teaching and Research Press,

Saussure F. 1983 (1916). *Course in General Linguistics.* (Trans. and ed.) by

Roy Harris. London: Duckworth.

Schachter, P. 1977. Constraints on coordinate structures. *Language* 53(1), 86 – 103.

Siewierska, Anna. 1988. *Word Order Rules.* London: Croom Helm.

Simone, R. (ed.). 1994. *Iconicity in Language.* Amsterdam: John Benjamins.

Slobin, Dan I. 1997. The Origins of Grammaticizable Notions: Beyond the Individual Mind. Dan I. Slobin (ed.). *The Crosslinguistic Study of Language Acquisition Vol. 5: Expanding the Contexts.* Mahwah, N. J., Lawrence Earlbaum Associates.

Sproat, R and C. Shin. 1988. Prenominal adjective orderings in English and Mandarin. *NELS* 18, 538 – 562.

Stucky, S. 1981. Free word order languages, free constituent order languages, and the gray area in between. *NELS* 11, 364 – 376.

Schmid, H-J. 2016. Why cognitive linguistics must embrace the social and pragmatic dimensions of language and how it could do so more seriously. *Cognitive Linguistics*, 27(4), 543 – 557.

Tabakowska, E. 1999. Linguistic Expression of Perceptual Relationships: Iconicity as a Principle of Text Organization. M. Nanny and O. Fischer (eds.). *Form Miming Meaning: Iconicity in Language and Literature*, 409 – 422. Amsterdam: John Benjamins.

Tai, J-H. Y. 1985. Temporal Sequence and Chinese Word Order. J. Haiman (ed.). *Iconicity in Syntax*, 49 – 73. Amsterdam: John Benjamins.

Tai, J-H. Y. 1988. Temporal sequence and word order in Chinese. *Foreign Linguistics* 1, 18 – 25.

Tai, J-H. Y. 1989. Toward a Cognition-based Functional Grammar of Chinese. J-H Tai and Frank Hsueh (eds.). *Functionalism and Chinese Grammar.* Chinese Language Teachers' Association Monograph Series. Vol. 1.

Tai, J-H. Y. 1995. Chinese grammar and bio-cognitive bases of human lan-

guage. *Journal of Chinese Linguistics*, 1999(13), 130 – 146.

Taylor, J. 1996. *Possessives in English: An Exploration in Cognitive Grammar.* Oxford: Clarendon Press.

Taylor, J. 2001. *Linguistic Categorization: Prototypes in Linguistic Theory.* Beijing: Foreign Language Teaching and Research Publishing Press.

Teyssier, J. 1968. Notes on the syntax of the adjectives in modern English. *Lingua* 20, 225 – 246.

Tomlin, R. S. 1985. Interaction of Subject, Theme, and Agent. J. Wirth (ed.). *Beyond the Sentence: Discourse and Sentential Form*, 61 – 80. Karoma Publishers, Ann Arbor.

Tomlin, R, S. 1986. *Basic Word Order: Functional Principles.* Great Britain: Mackays of Chatham, Kent.

Tomlin, R. and R. Rhodes. 1979. An introduction to information distribution in ojibwa. *Chicago Linguistics Society* 15, 307 – 320.

Traugott, Elizabeth C. and Charles A. Ferguson. 1982. *Toward a Checklist of Conditionals.* ms. Stanford University.

Traugott, Elizabeth C. 1985. Conditional Markers. J. Haiman (ed.) *Iconicity in Syntax.* Amsterdam: John Benjamins.

Ungerer, F and H. J. Schmid. 1996. *An Introduction to Cognitive Linguistics.* London: Longman.

van Dijk, A. and W. Kintsch. 1983. *Strategies of Discourse Comprehension.* New York: Academic Press.

van Valin, R. D. and R. J. Lapolla. 2002. *Syntax: Structure, Meaning and Function.* Beijing: Peking University.

Vendler, Z. 1968. Adjectives and Nominslizations. *Papers on Formal Linguistics. No.* 5. The Hague: Mouton.

Virtanen, T. 1992. *Discourse Functions of Adverbial Placement in English.* Åbo/

Turku: Åbo Akademi University Press.

Wakker, G. C. 1987. Purpose Clauses in Ancient Greek. J. Nuyts and G. de Schutter (eds.). *Getting One's Words into Line: On Word Order and Functional Grammar.* Functional Grammar series 5. Dordrecht, Holland, Providence, R. I.

Wang, Yin. 2001. *Semantics and Foreign Language Teaching.* Shanghai: Shanghai Foreign Language Teaching Press.

Weil, H. 1887. *The Order of Words in the Ancient Languages Compared with That of the Modern Languages.* Boston: Ginn.

Whitney, W. D. 1869. *Language and the Study of the Language.* New York: Scribner and Company.

Whorf, B. L. 1956. *Language, Thought, and Reality.* New York: Wiley.

Wierzbicka, A. 1990a. *The Semantics of Grammar.* Amsterdam: John Benjamins.

Wierzbicka, A. 1990b. The meaning of color terms: Semantics, culture and cognition. *Cognitive Linguistics* 1, 99 - 150.

Wolf, W. 2001. The Emergence of Experiential Iconicity and Spatial Perspective in Landscape Descriptions in English Fiction. F. Olga and M. Nanny (eds.). *The Motivated Sign: Iconicity in Langage and Literature*, 323 - 350. Amsterdam: John Benjamins.

Zadeh, L. A. 1965. Fuzzy Sets. *Information and Control* (8): 338 - 353.

Ziph, G. K. 1935. *The Psychobiology of Language.* New York: Houghton Mifflin.

Zhang, Gang. 1980. On word order. *Chinese Linguistics* 5, 348 - 349.

Zwicky, A. 1985. How to eescribe inflection. *Proceedings of the Eleventh Annual Meeting of the Berkeley Linguistics Society*, 372 - 386.

Zwicky, Arnold. 1986. German adjective agreement in GPSG. Linguistics 24 (5), 957 - 990.

白解红、秦茜茜. 2009. 英语名词短语中前置/后置修饰语选择的认知语义关系解释[J]. 邵阳学院学报, 8(1): 73 – 77.

陈存军. 1998. 论英语名词短语的定指性和指称性[J]. 解放军外国语学院学报, 21(5): 31 – 36.

曹炜. 2004. 汉英成对词比较研究[J]. 外语与外语教学, (1): 32 – 34.

程家枢、张云徽. 1989. 并列式双音复合名词的字序规律新探[J]. 云南教育学院学报, (1): 72 – 75.

鄂巧玲. 2001. 再谈并列双音词的字序[J]. 甘肃教育学院学报, (1): 63 – 65.

房玉清. 1992. 实用汉语语法[M]. 北京: 北京语言大学出版社.

顾嘉祖. 1986. 略谈英语形容词的词序问题[J]. 外国语, (2): 24 – 27.

郭绥龙. 1992. 现代英语表量限定词语用趋向[J]. 福建外语, 17 – 19.

高莉. 2010. 英汉运动动词词义合并对比研究[J]. 河北理工大学学报, 10(3): 138 – 140.

黄龙. 1986. 翻译技巧指导[M]. 沈阳: 辽宁人民出版社.

胡壮麟. 1997. 语言 认知 隐喻[J]. 现代外语, (4): 50 – 57.

李玲. 2001. 浅析英文的成对词[J]. 潍坊高等专科学校学报, (1): 82 – 83.

李雪. 2011. 汉英移动事件主体和参照物语言表达对比[J]. 外语教学与研究, 43(5): 689 – 701.

卢卫中. 2002. 词序的认知基础[J]. 解放军外国语学院学报, (5): 5 – 9.

陆丙甫. 2005. 语序优势的认知解释(上):论可别度对语序的普遍影响[J]. 当代语言学, 7(1): 1 – 15.

刘法公、张从孝. 1996. 汉英并列词语顺序比较与原理[J]. 外语与外语教学, (3): 31 – 34.

李冀宏、杨玉娟. 2008. 认知域与名词的可数性[J]. 外语教学, 29(4): 43 – 46.

马永田. 2014. 英语形名结构的认知研究[J]. 外语教学, (3):129 – 136.

秦裕祥．2008. 英语名词词组中前置修饰语使用限制的次范畴化解释[J]. 外语教学与研究，40(2)：113－120.

沈家煊．1993. 句法的象似性问题[J]. 外语教学与研究，(1)：2－8.

宋然然．2006. 语用层面的象似性考察[J]. 安徽农业大学学报，(1)：124－127.

威廉·冯·洪堡特．1999. 姚小平译．论人类语言结构的差异及其对人类精神发展的影响[M]. 北京：商务出版社．

威廉·冯·洪堡特．2011. 姚小平译．洪堡特语言哲学文集[M]. 北京：商务出版社．

汪德华．2002. 英语成对词语刍议[J]. 河南教育学院学报，(2)：151－152.

汪榕培．2002. 英语词汇学[M]. 上海：上海外语教育出版社．

王寅．1998. 标记象似性[J]. 外语学刊，(3)：10－15.

王寅．1999. 论语言符号象似性－对索绪尔任意说的挑战与补充[M]. 北京：新华出版社．

王寅．2000. 象似性：取得文体特征的重要手段[J]. 四川外语学院学报，(4)：39－43.

文旭．1999. 国外认知语言学研究纵观[J]. 外国语，(1)：34－40.

文旭．2000. 论语言符号的距离拟象性[J]. 外语学刊，(2)：71－74.

文旭．2001. 词序的拟象性探索[J]. 外语学刊，(3)：90－96.

王大鹏、曹井香．2008. 基于语料库的 DP 框架下英语后位限定词的排序分析[J]. 齐齐哈尔大学学报，(6)：101－103.

许国璋．1988. 语言符号的任意性问题[J]. 外语教学与研究，(3)：2－10.

张博．1996. 先秦并列式连用词序的制约机制[J]. 语言研究，(2)：13－26.

张敏．1998. 认知语言学与汉语名词短语[M]. 北京：中国社会科学出版社．

章振邦．1997. 新编英语语法概要[M]. 上海：上海外语教育出版社．

赵艳芳．2001. 认知语言学概论[M]. 上海：上海外语教育出版社．

祖生利 . 2002.《景德传灯录》中的联合式复音词[J]. 古汉语研究,(3):58 –63.

谢丽霞 . 2005. 英汉固定式成对词词序比较的认知研究(硕士研究生毕业论文). 湖南:湖南师范大学 .